20TH-CENTURY COMPOSERS

Jazz Greats

Jazz Greats

by David Perry

Φ

To my wife and principal editor, Jennifer, with my love.

Phaidon Press Limited
Regent's Wharf
All Saints Street
London N1 9PA

First Published 1996
© 1996 Phaidon Press Limited

ISBN 0 7148 3204 9

A CIP catalogue record for this book is
available from the British Library

Printed in Singapore

Frontispiece, in this 1949
photo, the tenor player Flip
Philips comes under the stern
scrutiny of Charlie Parker, the
most talented saxophonist in
the history of jazz.

Contents

Preface

I was fortunate that as a young employee of the BBC, I was allowed to follow some elaborate hunches and a deep-seated interest, and go off to make a series of jazz documentaries for Radio Three. This involved foolhardy treks across New Orleans in search of Buddy Bolden's home, and hair-raising trips up into Harlem or the South Bronx to seek out some long-forgotten witness to the early jazz era.

My colleague in the making of these programmes was Russell Davies, and I am grateful to him both for his unfailing good company and for the excellence of his jazz scholarship to which I feel a great debt.

I would like to thank the curators of the William Ransom Hogan Jazz Archive at the Tulane University in New Orleans for their help in making available the wealth of fascinating oral records that they have amassed.

I am grateful to the many jazz musicians I interviewed who were unfailingly courteous and helpful. One, Paul Barnes, who was close to death at the time of my visit showed me his fascinating hand-written diaries, while his wife cooked a meal of red beans and rice to welcome me to New Orleans. Often musicians and writers with a fearsomely militant or even anti-white reputation turned out to be the friendliest of all. In this respect I remember conversations with Max Roach and Amiri Baraka with particular pleasure.

Finally, I would like to thank Michael Berkeley for his advice on musical terminology, and Peter Owens of Phaidon Press for his sympathetic and perceptive editing.

David Perry
Knighton, Powys, 1995

I

An army band of the Civil War era. For many southern blacks, emancipation from slavery became associated with military music played by the Union forces.

We are done with hoeing cotton
We are done with hoeing corn.
We are coloured Yankee soldiers
As sure as you are born.
When Masse hears us shouting
He will think 'tis Gabriel's horn
As we go marching on.

A version of *The Battle Hymn of the Republic* sung by freed slaves who joined the Union Army in the American Civil War

The Origins of Jazz

Jazz music, which emerged in the United States around the turn of the century, came to the attention of Europeans for the first time in 1917. In April of that year, America declared war on Germany and among the troops sent across the Atlantic to fight in the French and Belgian battlefields were several thousand black soldiers. Some of them used the military instruments they brought with them to experiment with new jazz ideas whenever they got the chance, others carried in their kit the first primitive gramophone recordings of jazz. The vitality of this original musical idiom made a powerful impact in the trenches, but it was not always a positive one. The great English war poet, Wilfred Owen, wrote a letter in 1917 in which he listed, in a light-hearted way, the things he most disliked about life in the trenches and which he would banish forever when the war was over. Jazz music was a prominent item. Sadly, Owen was spared jazz music and all his other pet hates because he died in action the following year.

Black Americans serving in the United States Army, photographed at Auteuil, France, during the First World War. It was soldiers like these who brought the first jazz records to Europe in 1917.

After the war, many Europeans, already primed by a craze for ragtime music and the cakewalk dance, were generally fascinated by the new musical form. Some prominent black bands used jazz elements in their acts, and were well placed to capitalize on this mood. Chief among these was the thirty-five piece orchestra of Will Marion Cook which undertook a European tour in 1919. In the clarinet section was a young New Orleans musician of instinctive brilliance called Sidney Bechet, and in the audience for one of their concerts was the distinguished Swiss conductor, Ernest Ansermet. He was so impressed by Bechet's music that he set down these thoughts in a periodical called the *Revue romande*.

[Bechet] is the first of his race to have composed perfectly formed blues on the clarinet … their form was gripping, abrupt, harsh, with a brusque and pitiless ending like that of Bach's Second Brandenburg Concerto … His art is perhaps the highway the whole world will swing along tomorrow.

Ansermet was wrong about Bechet being 'the first of his race …' but quite right to emphasize the importance of American blacks in the creation of jazz. And by describing Bechet's solos as compositions, the conductor implicitly acknowledged his surprise that an instinctive non-reading musician could achieve such perfection of form.

For neither Bechet nor any other of the great jazz musicians in this book was a composer in the sense that we understand Shostakovich or Schoenberg to be composers. For much of its history little or no jazz music has been written down. This is not just an historical oddity but a crucial element in how jazz was formed, and what jazz became. Someone who heard the first stirrings of jazz in the streets of New Orleans was the conventionally-trained Creole cornetist, Peter Bocage. He believed the new musical idiom was born precisely because there were a lot of musicians in the city who could play but not read: 'They made up their own music, and they played it their own way, you understand?' In other words, faced with a musical notation they did not understand, American blacks simply went their own way and relied on their wits.

Jazz has remained predominantly a music of group and individual improvisation ever since. For the most part, jazz musicians composed on their feet, sometimes in front of noisy, even violent, demanding crowds. Ansermet's comments on Bechet's playing were shot through with a sense of the revolutionary impact of jazz. Later, Leonard Bernstein was to call it 'the only original American art form' – a big claim. The technique of improvisational composition contributed to the unique musical qualities that so impressed these listeners, and improvisational composition was an indirect consequence of the African origins of those who 'invented' jazz.

Descendants of plantation slaves, it is argued, fused what they had kept alive of their African musical heritage with American military marches and dance tunes to create a new form of musical expression. In broad terms this is true, but it takes a little detective work to pin down exactly how these two traditions inter-reacted.

Slaves in the American southern states kept the flame of African music alive from generation to generation. It was probably a private activity, confined to slave quarters after the day's work was over and making use of anything that came to hand as instruments. Such music-making was a solace and escape, a way of dealing with the devastating trauma of capture and transportation across the ocean to America. On many plantations it would not have been discouraged – some enlightened masters probably took an interest. Music was only one element in the sophisticated world the slaves made; cooking and linguistic play also nourished an ancestral memory of their African homeland.

Opposite, cotton pickers' quarters in Arkansas, where the subjugation of rural blacks continued until long after the era of slavery. Such places bred the work song, the holler and the blues.

What characterized the West African musical traditions that the slaves nurtured? African music is a vast subject, but when it comes to the origins of jazz there are several elements that seem to have been particularly influential: a highly developed sense of rhythm and counter rhythm, more complex than that heard in most European music; the paramount importance of the voice, not only for story-telling, but as the carrier of emotion; and an inherited five-tone scale which, once learned, made the thirds and sevenths of the traditional European scale difficult to master. The five-tone scale was not unique to Africa and can be encountered in some forms of European folk music, most notably in the gypsy tradition of Slovakia and Rumania (incidentally, one of the greatest European jazz innovators, the guitarist Django Reinhardt, was of gypsy stock). This has led some writers to question the importance of the African origins of jazz.

However, it is not just historical romanticism, but common sense that suggests that the slaves' use of the five-tone scale derived from Africa.

By the early nineteenth century many white Americans had become fascinated by the black sub-culture they found in their midst and composers started to produce songs that imitated slave music from the plantations. African polyrhythms and scales were hinted at by the incorporation of gentle syncopation and a playful use of the melodic colouring of work songs. Plantation songs became extremely popular and composers such as Stephen Foster acquired nationwide fame.

The importance of this genre in preparing the way for jazz has been underrated because of the sentimental attitude to slavery that it betrayed and the thoroughly bowdlerized version of black music that it projected. It is hardly surprising that the view of slavery taken by songwriters who were rooted in the ethos of the slave era should be profoundly unsympathetic to us today, but in their own very imperfect way these composers were expressing interest in slaves and even sympathy for their plight. Plantation songs brought a version of black music into the mainstream of American popular culture for the first time, and started a tradition of musical cross-fertilization which helped prepare the way for jazz.

Of course, being the focus of white interest which was often confused and laden with preconceptions was painful for many blacks, but it undoubtedly influenced the way they projected themselves. A black tradition of minstrel singing and clowning arose, in which negroes, to some extent, played up to the image put upon them by whites. Before working up a lather of political righteousness about the eye-rolling and crowd-pleasing antics on which Louis Armstrong built his stage act, it would be as well to reflect on their genesis in this very real minstrel tradition.

After emancipation in 1865, itinerant black pianists like Scott Joplin enlivened saloons and dance halls throughout the USA's south and south-west with a lively dance music based on a bright two beats to the bar rhythm and jagged, boldly delineated melodies. It became known as 'ragged time', a term which referred to the contrast between the highly syncopated melody and the rhythmically regular bass line. Ragged time became corrupted to 'ragtime' and the name stuck. This genre may have developed from black banjo music played by privileged slaves when they were invited into the owner's house to provide evening entertainment.

Joplin and others started to notate their best known pieces, and some, like *Maple Leaf Rag* became hits, and would eventually provide the basis for the first jazz improvisations. Once the sheet music was published, orchestral ragtime established itself. Piano, bass, guitar and drums played the rhythmic background, while the melody was assigned to a couple of violins, or cornet or two, a flute, a clarinet and a trombone.

Ragtime was the music of well-placed educated blacks who were able to take their chance when emancipation came. Some of them would have been made freemen before that time, by grateful or liberal owners. The blues, on the other hand, spoke uncompromisingly of the venality of the contract between white landowner and black labourer. When it comes to the origin of the blues, we are in the realm of historic conjecture. It seems likely that they emerged in the Mississippi Delta around the time of emancipation, and developed from the call and response of the slaves' group work song, an expression of solidarity and mutual support. The twelve bars of the classic blues were divided into two verses, each of three lines. The first two lines were identical and the third was end-rhymed with them. The rasping vocal tone of the lone blues singer, often produced from deep in the back of the throat, derived from another slave utterance: 'the holler', a primitive expression of suffering and despair.

The subjects of the blues were faithless lovers, exile, the grind of hard labour, poverty and hunger. The clinching rhyme in the third line of each verse provided no resolution and only served to enhance the feeling of despair.

The melodic oddity of the blues was probably the result of the African scale encountering the European scale. Slaves were taught hymns as soon as they were settled on a plantation. This rather bizarre meeting of minds meant that faced with a European third or seventh, the slave sang an off note which became known as a 'blue note'. The effect of melancholy and longing produced by this musical accident perfectly suited the message of the blues.

The final element in the mosaic of proto-jazz musical styles was the marching band which became so important in black communities after the Civil War in the 1860s. They played standards like Henry

Bishop's *Home Sweet Home* and Septimus Winner's *Listen to the Mockingbird* in a style that was cacophonous, rough and yet rhythmically stirring. Cornets, trombones, clarinets, alto and baritone saxophones and tuba played parallel melodic lines that sometimes produced an accidental polyphony, while a battery of snare and bass drums with cymbal attached, brought up the rear.

The marching bands with their smartly uniformed musicians became associated with funeral processions, playing dirges on the way to the cemetry and lively marches on the way back. There was nothing self-conscious about these bands. In fact, what they demonstrated was that the memory of an African past was being submerged temporarily by the vision of an American future. By submitting themselves to the discipline of the two- or four-beat bar of the standards of the day, the blacks could not have been further from the subtle and complex polyrhythmic instincts of their African ancestors. It was a way of adapting to the new culture in which they

Marching outfits like the Holmes band sprang up all over Louisiana in the late nineteenth century. New Orleans was the centre for such music, which became an important precursor of jazz.

found themselves, and in a sense, it was an act of faith in the
possibility of becoming integrated into a white America. Hopes for a
life of dignity and prosperity ran high after the emancipation and
these feelings could be condemned as naive only with hindsight.

The most significant centre of marching band activity in the
American south was the city of New Orleans, which was an
important military as well as commercial port throughout the
ninteenth century. The second-hand military band instruments that
helped spawn marching bands were widely available and cheap.
Bearing grandiloquent names such as the Excelsior Brass Band or the
Magnolia Brass Band, they would parade through streets of elegant
stucco houses with ornate wrought iron balconies, built in the rigid
grid system that betrayed the eighteenth-century French origins of the
city. In their way these streets were the architectural embodiment of
the iron musical discipline of the two- or four-beat bar.

But it was not just marching bands that could be heard in New
Orleans. By the second half of the nineteenth century it had become
the music capital of the New World. Creole orchestras such as John
Robichaux's played elegant ragtime in the parks, and minstrel shows
and plantation songs could be enjoyed in downtown theatres. There
were three symphony orchestras, and a wide range of European folk
music brought over by immigrants, while from the Mississippi, the
sound of the riverboat steam calliope floated across the city.

New Orleans was not surrounded by today's urban sprawl of
shopping malls and conference centres and the aural impact of all this
on the rural labourers who worked on the Mississippi levee, close to
the elegant churches and boulevards of the old city, must have been
dramatic and beguiling. For the same reason, the city for all its
musical sophistication was strongly rooted in the blues tradition of
the surrounding countryside, the sounds of which would have drifted
into its streets and squares.

This musical relationship between rural primitivism and urban
sophistication was formalized by regular Sunday gatherings at the
city's Congo Square. Here, New Orleanians could gather and listen to
unreconstituted rural folk music with unsubdued African elements,
sung and played by plantation workers. This tradition went right
back to the slave era when part of Sunday was set aside for music-
making in the city. New arrivals from Africa were particularly

A bird's eye view of New Orleans engraved by John Wells in 1870, with paddle steamers on the Mississippi, and Lake Pontchartrain in the background.

encouraged to sing and play. It seems likely that the Congo Square gatherings played an important part in keeping the flame of African music alight in New Orleans until it flared up triumphantly with the creation of jazz music.

The city also had a social history that marked it out from other big towns of the American south, and which was also conducive to the creation of jazz music because it engendered black pride. New Orleans was founded by the French in 1718 and until the Louisiana Purchase of 1803 when the USA acquired the territory, political and social rights in the city were based on the establishment of a line of descent from the original settler rather than on colour. This meant that a wealthy caste of Creoles (people of mixed race whose culture was French) established itself. For the white French, cultural pride proved a stronger prejudice than racial antipathy so anyone who could speak the language fluently or appreciate fine cooking was perceived as in some way an honorary French citizen. And if there was negro blood, so be it.

Jelly Roll Morton, the self-proclaimed inventor of jazz, photographed at a piano in Chicago in 1926

Although the American system swiftly eroded the social standing of the Creoles as the nineteenth century progressed, a shabby sophistication persisted, and a ghost of their French past haunted many in the city. When rural blacks from the hinterland began to trickle into New Orleans to find work, this sophistication, although faded and marooned in a dying past, gave the newcomers something to which they could aspire.

But, more than anything, it was the heady mixture of musical styles to be heard in New Orleans at the turn of the century that made it the birthplace of jazz. It was like the rich variety of cuisines – French, Caribbean, Cajun, Black American – which could also be enjoyed in the city. Chefs at top restaurants, like Antoine's, took elements from all these traditions to create a new style of cooking, unique to New Orleans. But who would emerge as the musical chefs, capable of using the city's musical cultures as the ingredients in an altogether new form?

Opposite, Morton had a flair for self-promotion. By publishing his compositions at a time when many contemporaries were just improvising on tunes they had heard, he ensured his name would be remembered.

According to Jelly Roll Morton's none-too-modest account recorded by historians in the 1930s, he was responsible for inventing jazz single-handedly in 1902. The Creole pianist was, he says, playing a rag in the customary two beat to the bar rhythm, when he suddenly had the idea that he could generate a lot of excitement

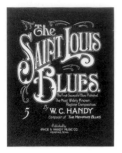

W. C. Handy's *St Louis Blues* became one of the great jazz standards.

by simultaneously stomping his foot at four beats to the bar. However ludicrous the idea that one man, or one simple rhythmic idea could create jazz, the undergirding of two-beat marches and rags with a four/four ground beat was important in creating a new, infectious sort of music. The early players referred to it as 'hot' music, and the term jazz was not coined until later. A white bass player called Steve Brown, who was working in New Orleans just around the turn of the century, remembered that in the new style *St Louis Blues* would be played in four/four time, while in ragtime it would be played in two/four time.

There was another simultaneous process at work which was more organic and mysterious than doubling up the beat. It was the inflection of ragtime with blues elements. The jazz pioneers discovered that the hitherto stiff-sounding clarinet and cornet could be released into a new idiom. By bending notes, growling, calling and delaying entrances they made their instruments talk, as if in imitation of the African vocal tradition so well preserved in the blues.

Above all it was the injection of African rhythm into European forms that gave jazz its defining idiom. As we have seen, the first black marching bands embraced the discipline of strict European rhythms partly out of a sense of social optimism. The first jazz players undercut the symmetry of the 'hot' music they had created out of marches and rags by juxtaposing its four beat to the bar pulse with the complexities of African polyrhythms. The regular European beat provided a framework within which the African rhythmic spirit could be explored. Cornet and clarinet, the carriers of the melody, danced in and out of the regular beat marked by bassist, drummer and guitarist, using them like counterparts in a rhythmic conversation.

This musical idea gained some of its power from the fact that it encapsulated the social situation of American blacks whose African soul was trapped, as it were, in a social system devised by and for whites. And just as this subject people moved slowly and painfully from the shadow of slavery towards civil rights, so the African rhythmic elements in the jazz equation become ever more liberated and complex. Although contemporary drummers like Max Roach and Elvin Jones use each hand and foot independently to mark four separate rhythms simultaneously, they have not lost touch with their roots. Roach often uses the high hat cymbal to mark a two beat to the bar pulse rising above the complexity, and echoing exactly the two beat to the bar clash of the hand cymbals used in the old New Orleans marching bands.

For the first jazz musicians, the idea that African rhythms working against European rhythms might have social and racial implications was almost certainly instinctive rather than conscious, and there was nothing strident about it. In an earlier era, looking at Beaumarchais' pre-revolutionary play *The Marriage of Figaro*, Napoleon observed that it was as if the revolution was already quietly happening. In the same way, with hindsight, the early history of jazz could be construed as an embryonic Civil Rights movement. The courage with which musicians faced segregated audiences speaks volumes for their dignity, inner strength and sheer endurance. In this context the elements of improvisation and group co-operation that characterized jazz musically, became a sort of political device, a self-help mechanism for people who are up against it. This idea is born out by a fascinating recent episode in the history of the music. In Poland and Russia in the 1970s, before the first glimpses of *glasnost*, jazz became extremely popular, symbolizing personal liberty and solidarity when faced with oppression.

Parades like this were provoked by the wave of black lynchings that occurred throughout the south in the early 1920s. Jazz musicians did not adopt an explicit stance on civil rights until the late 1920s, but their music exuded black pride.

The rhythmic felicity which is at the heart of jazz has its root in the creative clash of African and European rhythmic traditions. The word 'swing' was not coined until 1930 but the playing of early Armstrong, Bechet and we can assume, Bolden, certainly swung in just the sense that the word was invented to describe. Jazz was not the first Afro-European musical hybrid, but its predecessors did not create a comparable impact. The plantation song was too much at the mercy of its own notions about slavery and presented a pastoral version of life in the rural south of America. The blues, though powerful, was too primitive in its form and means of expression – solo voice and plucked guitar – to grip a mass audience. And while ragtime was highly successful, the syncopation of the melody was formulaic, a predictable device. The swing of jazz, on the other hand, was like a living thing, a virus – albeit a benign one – that before long was to grip the whole of America.

From the outset the approach of jazz players was instinctive and spontaneous. The first signs of improvised melody could be heard in the breaks played by front-line musicians in the marching bands. These were unaccompanied extemporizations lasting just two or four bars. Such primitive breaks were exchanged by Louis Armstrong and King Oliver and captured on the 1923 recordings of Oliver's great band. A quarter of a century later Charlie Parker, the be-bop saxophonist, had extended the break so as to display the incandescent creativity of his alto playing.

But, typically, as players became more confident, breaks were extended into choruses, and group improvisation filled in behind as accompaniment. The term 'chorus' in the jazz context does not mean a repeated refrain as it does in the case of a song or hymn, but any statement or restatement with variations of a theme. Improvisation really got under way with the rough polyphony of the early New Orleans jazz bands in which cornet, clarinet and trombone played interweaving lines of melody over the rhythmic accompaniment of tuba, or double bass (usually bowed), drums, guitar and sometimes piano. There were few solos. Well known rags and blues were the primary material that jazz musicians used as their starting point. As the music developed Tin Pan Alley hits and Gershwin numbers were also explored for their harmonic and melodic possibilities. From its early years, jazz was like a pinch of yeast that enlivened sometimes

stale American popular songs. Old numbers could be transformed by
jazz, as if by alchemy. When avant-garde jazz players finally turned
their back on Tin Pan Alley as a source of musical material in the
1960s, a half a century of fruitful tradition was ended.

Out of the New Orleans ensemble emerged the solos of Louis
Armstrong in the late 1920s. Then the big bands became
predominant in the 1930s. With their dramatic and contrapuntal use
of instrumental 'choirs' big band leaders like Duke Ellington and
Count Basie made creative use of the riff – a repeating melody of two
or four bars with its origins in the call and response of African music,
and which had appeared both in blues and marching band music.
Once the riff was established in one section of the band, harmonic
variations could be played over it to great effect.

After the swing era the small 'combo' or combination re-emerged,
and led directly to be-bop with its burry ensembles of trumpet
and saxophone, strange inside-out harmonies and lithe asymmetrical
melodies. The marking of rhythm became highly fragmented and
oblique, with the pianist improvising a chordal accompaniment
behind the soloist in an arhythmic, taunting way, the drummer playing against the beat as often as with it, and only the bassist holding
a regular pulse.

When free jazz emerged in the 1960s the idea of a regular pulse
was thrown out altogether. But in other respects, free jazz was closer
to the group improvisation of New Orleans, with everyone playing
at once and only the most basic of structural and harmonic
guidelines pertaining.

Charlie Parker's name is invariably invoked as the pre-eminent
improvisational composer in the history of jazz. He was a musician
of such protean fecundity that he was incapable of playing the same
solo twice. The way he seamlessly incorporated little formulaic
devices or 'licks' into his choruses was brilliant. There followed
Ornette Coleman, a modernist saxophonist who spent three years
studying the violin and the trumpet precisely because they were alien
to him, and offered him no easy musical solutions. Coleman's belief
was that every solo should be approached with a mind which was
'tabula rasa' – completely blank. However, such fundamentalist
improvisation is rare in jazz, much rarer than is assumed. Some of
the finest improvisations took the form of melodic paraphrases – a

slight hesitation here, an unusual emphasis there, and the whole thing was transformed – Louis Armstrong was a master of this.

Moreover, an improvisational idea, once arrived at could be repeated without any loss of fervour. The saxophonist Greely Walton had the good fortune to hear Louis Armstrong and Joe Oliver playing together in their famous 1920s residency at the Lincoln Gardens, Chicago. Walton recalled the brilliance of the music, but added that the arrangements and solos were more or less the same night after night. Interestingly, one of the early New Orleans terms for an improvisor was a 'routine player'. Presumably the 'routine' disguised the lack of reading ability.

So improvisation in jazz need not be highly original. Conversely, assumptions about the 'European' approach of composers like Duke Ellington, and with them the resultant problem of explaining their jazz credentials, are equally askew. When Duke's son, Mercer, went through his father's papers after the great man's death, he was hoping to find some of the arrangements for the hundreds of numbers Duke had put his name to. To his astonishment, Mercer found that there were none, just a few primitive jottings on yellowing score paper.

In fact, Ellington's approach was not so very different from that of Oliver and Armstrong at the Lincoln Gardens. Duke's music was always inspired by the individual attack and style of the great soloists who worked with him. And as he once said when asked how arranged music could be jazz: 'No one ever played a good solo without thinking about it first.'

So where does this leave the idea of improvisational composition? Perhaps the key to jazz playing is something that might be termed 'improvisational attack', an approach which could be perpetually renewed or repeated, but which was always imbued with an informal tone and a personal feeling. Again, this goes back to the African remnants at the heart of jazz, and the way European instruments were given a vocal, human character. And it all started in the turn-of-the-century New Orleans with a man who knew only that he was a 'routine player' because he could not read a note of music.

2

A portrait of Buddy Bolden
from 1895, a couple of
years before he recorded a
cylinder, which has never
been found

*I attribute it all to Bolden you know. Because
of the simple fact that Bolden was a fellow – he
didn't know a note as big as a house, if you
understand what I mean. And whatever they
played, they made it up you see. It was
improvisation, you see.*

Peter Bocage, New Orleans cornetist,
interviewed in 1975

Buddy Bolden

For a long time there was much legend surrounding the man who was said to have been the first jazz player. The magical city of New Orleans had produced an equally magical musician to mark the birth of its jazz lineage in the shape of Buddy Bolden. Bolden, it was said, was the descendant of a West African king; when he played, on a clear night the sound of his cornet carried for twelve miles right across the Mississippi delta; he was a barber, and for light relief, he edited a newsheet called *The Cricket*.

There was a great deal of licence in all this, and Bolden seems to attract myths like a honey pot attracts bees, for one very good reason: none of his music was preserved. The lack of any musical evidence is all the more tantalizing for jazz scholars because there is a reliable report that Bolden's band did record a cylinder just before the turn of the century. Bolden's trombonist, Willie Cornish, had a clear memory of this, but no one has ever been able to locate the cylinder. It has to be said that even if this grail-like object did turn up in some dusty New Orleans basement, the recording would be almost totally inaudible by now.

So we have to reconstruct Bolden's music imaginatively, using the wide range of first-hand reports of his playing that have survived. There is certainly enough evidence to suggest that it was Buddy Bolden who played the first recognizable jazz music to be heard on the streets of New Orleans.

The register of births and deaths in the city reveals that Buddy was born on 6 September 1877, twelve years after the abolition of slavery. He was the son of a drayman called Westmore Bolden, who died of pneumonia when Buddy was just six. An older sister had already died, and Buddy, his mother Alice and his remaining younger sister Cora, stayed close for the rest of their lives.

They were a poor, respectable family, who took great comfort from their Baptist faith. The Boldens worshipped to the gospel stomp, with singing and hand-clapping of such vigour that the whole church shook to the beat. These buildings were flimsy, wooden affairs, casually set down on some empty lot, and there was a report in the *Daily Picayune* in 1889 that one such church was literally shifted off its foundations by the sheer athleticism of its worshippers.

Inspired by the power of gospel music, Buddy wanted to learn more. Somehow his mother found the money for him to take cornet lessons when he was a teenager with a cook called Manuel Hall, a friend of the family. Buddy learned fast and before long he joined a small dance band, led by a guitar player called Charlie Galloway, which was probably a version of ragtime bands of the time incorporating cornet, violin, flute and trombone. Galloway was the real barber of the Bolden legend, not Bolden himself. The backroom of his salon, a cool and dark sanctuary from the fierce New Orleans heat, would have been a congenial place to practise, drink, or just talk about the musical scene. It was popular with New Orleans musicians, who would drop in for a haircut and then make a little music afterwards. One of those who did this with some regularity was a clarinet player called Frank Lewis, whom Bolden would later hire when he came to form his own band.

Buddy soon began to feel constrained by his musical apprenticeship, and sensed he should move on. He was a confident but impatient young man, with a good technical grasp of the cornet, and his desire to play was insatiable. Before long he left the seductive but slightly complacent charms of Galloway's barber's salon and established his own band.

There is a famous photograph, taken around 1900, when Buddy was about twenty-three, of the line-up that he put together. Buddy on cornet, Willie Cornish on valve trombone, Frank Lewis and Willie Warner on clarinets, Brock Mumford on guitar and Jimmy Johnson on bowed bass (the fashion for plucked bass did not start until later). No drummer appears on the photograph and no-one really knows why not, because Buddy always used drums. Perhaps his regular drummer, Cornelius Tillman was still sleeping off a particularly late and heavy night of music-making when this haunting picture was taken. Haunting because it provides such a clear visual record of the first jazz band in history but is, of course, mute. It is posed in the typical static style of the day, with the musicians addressing their instruments formally. In this way it seems to evoke silence rather than

The Bolden family home from 1887 until 1905 was at 2309 First Street, New Orleans. The house is now a city landmark.

Following page, The Bolden band, about 1900. Standing from left: Willie Warner (clarinet), Willie Cornish (valve trombone), Buddy Bolden, Jimmy Johnson (bass). Sitting from left: Frank Lewis (clarinet), Brock Mumford (guitar). Bolden's drummer missed the photo call.

the musical passion we associate with Buddy Bolden. Bolden himself was a stocky, deep-chested figure, with confident, intelligent eyes. As if to demonstrate his self-assurance he called his outfit Buddy Bolden's Band, eschewing the impersonal and grandiloquent names adopted by the black marching bands of the time. But, like most marching band musicians, the members of Bolden's outfit were improvisers, none of them read music – they copied, learned and changed what they heard. What Bolden achieved he achieved unconsciously, instinctively, almost unknowingly. A musical naif, it was precisely his lack of formal musical training that helped engender jazz music. The cornetist Peter Bocage put it simply when he remarked, 'I attribute it all to Bolden, you know … [and] he didn't know a note as big as a house, if you understand what I mean.'

The earliest public performance by Bolden remembered with any clarity was in a different context. He was working in the front line of a New Orleans marching band. It was 1898, and the Spanish-American War had just started. Troops and bandsmen were gathering at the New Orleans quayside ready to embark on the transport ships to Cuba. They were in high spirits, having been led to believe by the powers that be that Cuba was a veritable paradise where the streams flowed with rum, and beautiful women wore flowers in their hair. All they had to do was to win the war and all this was theirs. To capitalize on the party mood, and to keep the troops' spirits buoyed up until they were safely at sea, it was decided that a marching band would give the boys a rousing musical send-off.

So Bolden and his uniformed band positioned themselves at the water's edge ready to play. But when they struck up, it was not with the sort of patriotic or sinew-stiffening stuff that the military authorities might have hoped for, but with the popular Victorian tear-jerker, *Home Sweet Home*.

The future bandleader Ray Lopez was at the quayside, 'I'm telling you there was more banjos coming over the side of that transport, over the side the boys went, they just couldn't take it. Banjos and violins floating in that river for a week. They jumped over and swam before the boat got too far out in the river. That *Home Sweet Home* hit them. And women with all their shouting and screaming and laughing, they starts crying, screaming and crying, you see.'

Home Sweet Home was a standard of the marching band repertoire, but to play it on this occasion was a stroke of mischievous genius, whether conscious or unconscious. *Home Sweet Home* was not just a subversive way of undermining the soldiers' will to go to Cuba, it was also a tribute to Bolden's lost homeland of Africa – and to the many conscripted black soldiers on the transport boat, the point would not have been lost.

Bolden's choice of tune, and the mutiny and pandemonium it created made a small piece of American military history. As Ray Lopez remarked, 'I understand that from that day to this the army does not allow them ever to play *Home Sweet Home* at a send off.' *Home Sweet Home* was not yet jazz. But Bolden's genius for playing the right tune at the right time – or the wrong tune at the wrong time – and the power of his cornet playing had combined to turn a familiar standard into a call to mutiny.

The Spanish-American war was over before 1898 was out, and the musical fever that was gripping New Orleans was heightened by the large numbers of military cornets, banjos and drums that came onto the market when the troops were discharged. Everybody sensed that a new music was in the offing and musicians were experimenting with the redundant instruments. Bolden's career was definitely on the move now, and with the band he had assembled he started to build a repertory of numbers more amenable to the rhythmic and melodic style that interested him.

When his band played at dances in the long narrow wooden huts with corrugated iron roofs that were used as working mens' halls in New Orleans, the impact was as powerful as that of Baptist worship at its most fervent, or voodoo at its most beguiling. The sexually suggestive *Make me a Pallet on Your Floor* was typical of the sort of number Bolden was playing in the early years of the century. It had a bright, raggy melody inflected with a strong strain of melancholy, imported from the blues tradition.

At some point around this time Bolden must have discovered the doubling up of the two-beat ragtime rhythm that Morton described. William Ridgely, a black trombonist of the time, remembers Bolden playing a two-beat to the bar ragtime rhythm. But Bill Matthews, a teenage drummer in Bolden's heyday recalled the powerful effect of Buddy's hot rhythm on his audience. 'The women would be jumping out of the windows, jumping out shouting, Buddy Bolden – he's wonderful!' It seems likely that Bolden made the transition to hot rhythm around 1902, precisely the year that Morton claimed to have invented jazz. When his band mastered the new idiom, the four beat bar marked by drums, guitar and bowed bass provided a sort of rhythmic drone. The clarinets of Frank Lewis and Willie Warner put up an eerie banshee wail while Bolden and Cornish skipped in and out of the rhythm with powerful and expressive playing that seemed to be hypnotic. Bolden could whip up a frenzy in the crowd, especially the women, that was partly religious, partly sexual. His cornet playing was not only incomparably powerful, but could be sweet, low, menacing or vibrant. Its intensely vocalized idiom evoked echoes of the singing of his African ancestors. Bolden was the first cornet player to master this idiom which was so crucial to the development of jazz. For Bill Matthews his playing was a revelation. 'Buddy Bolden was one of the heaviest, loudest trumpet player [sic] that ever was in New Orleans … Old slow, low down blues, he had a moan in his cornet – it goes all through you just like when you go to church or something. Just tell those boys get low. When he say "Get low" and he takes it …'

The Union Sons Hall in Perdido Street, where Bolden enthralled his audiences, became known as Funky Butt Hall, after Bolden's famous song.

Jazz started as dance music and that social function was crucial
in forming its character. Its birth coincided with the new interest in
sexually oriented, informal dancing that began at the turn of the
century in America, and had reached epidemic proportions by the
1920s. But as the music became more sophisticated this primal link
with dancing became a burden. For Duke Ellington, the problem was
practical: how to keep churning out dance numbers when he also
wanted to produce more ambitious pieces. By the time Charlie Parker
came along in the late 1940s, it became a matter of principle to
divorce the modernist art of be-bop from dancing altogether. The
vehemence with which Parker reacted against the idea of jazz as
dance music was in itself evidence of the enduring power of the link.
For Bolden there were no such hang-ups.

Bolden's primitive jazz seemed to be capable of suffusing a
mundane, even sordid social event with powerful transcendant
emotion. Here again the African origins of jazz could be discerned.
West African music had precisely the same sort of roots in daily
rituals and the same intense, spiritual feeling: it was a much less
dualistic musical tradition than that of Europe. And as jazz developed
there was often the whiff of religious rites about it. In a jam session
players display a sort of exaggerated modesty towards each other as if
reluctant to impose themselves. Even a player's testing of a mouthpiece before stepping forward to take a solo, is carried out in a highly
stylized ritualistic way. The audience is invited to get involved by
clapping, shouting and so on. The whole thing is reminiscent of West
African dance ceremonies and black American church services.

It is not difficult to imagine the sweaty, fetid atmosphere that built
up in the small airless dance halls on steamy summer nights. Indeed,
one song Bolden played celebrated the very real physical presence
of his adoring audience. The song was called *Funky Butt, Funky Butt,
Take it Away* – 'funky' meaning smelly, and 'butt' meaning behind.
Willie Cornish explained in an interview late in his life that he came
up with the tune during a particularly hot night in the halls. 'Open
up those windows, And let that bad air out' the lyric pleaded. Most of
the other words are unprintable. This Rabelaisian number devised by
his trombonist became Bolden's calling card in the area around
Rampart and Perdido Streets where he did most of his work. Many
years later this song was to be transformed into *Buddy Bolden's Blues*

by the suave, self-appointed and sometimes self-serving historian of
New Orleans jazz, Jelly Roll Morton. Morton was determined to leave
his fingerprints on anything to do with the origins of jazz and the
Funky Butt song was no exception.

Around 1904, as Bolden's confidence and reputation grew, he took
his music to the more genteel milieu of Johnson Park where a mixed
crowd used to gather to hear the elegant Creole orchestra led by
John Robichaux. As far as Bolden was concerned, Robichaux was
yesterday's man and he set out to prove it. He set himself up in a
bandstand at the opposite side of the park and started to play with his
usual vigour and hot rhythm. At climactic moments Bolden would
thrust his cornet out of the bandstand window and play with searing
power towards the crowd listening to Robichaux. As Bolden's ecstatic,
unpredictable tones floated across the night air, the crowd, keen to
hear this new music at close quarters, could not help but drift away
from the rather arthritic articulations of Robichaux's ragtime. Bolden's
friend, Louis Jones, interviewed in extreme old age, remembered that
Buddy was delighted by the outcome 'That's why Buddy Bolden used
to say to Cornish, "Come on, put your hands through the window,
'cos I'm going to call my children home."'

This striking scene as Bolden 'called his children home' with all the
primitive power of a voodoo priest, marks the time when jazz music
first found its voice with complete confidence. Bolden was dubbed
King Bolden. Nothing to do with the royal rulers of Benin, but an
acknowledgment that he was the best, the first in a series of charismatic horn players to bewitch the people of New Orleans. The crown
would pass from Buddy Bolden to Buddy Petit, to Freddie Keppard
to Joe Oliver and finally to Louis Armstrong before this archaic New
Orleans line of kings was to peter out.

Everyone agreed on the power of Bolden's playing, and no doubt
John Robichaux would have attested to it also. It is easy to see how the
'twelve miles on a clear night' legend arose. New Orleans is built on
marshy land and this, together with the river and the proximity of a
couple of lakes, plays tricks with sound. In those traffic-free days it
was probably possible to catch fragments of Bolden's solos as they
carried to different corners of the city and to go along with the myth
of his almost god-like power.

What Buddy Bolden's Baptist mother and sister would have made of songs like *Funky Butt* or the even more scandalous, *If You Don't Shake, You Don't Get No Cake*, we can only guess. Bolden was leading a fast life, drinking heavily, and cashing in on his manifest ability to drive women mad with his music, in a series of stage-door liaisons that would not have shamed a 1960s pop star. Indeed, Bolden seems to have started an unfortunate tradition among jazz musicians for fast and destructive living. For a while he seems to have kept going by separating his professional life from his home life, and by treating the family house at 2309 First Street as a sort of sanctuary.

Certainly, there's a sense of neighbourly peacefulness when you visit the Bolden home, miraculously still standing in a modest, respectable black neighbourhood which seems almost unchanged since Buddy's time. The houses are constructed very simply out of wood, with ornamental panels running along the eaves. The monotony of the design is relieved by bright and cheerful colours, and flowering shrubs in pots bring vibrant life to the small yards.

An attractive aspect of the New Orleans of Bolden's time was the way in which poor neighbourhoods like his were as integral to the city as the magnificent white-porticoed and magnolia-swamped mansions of the Garden City district. Better-off blacks than Bolden would have lived in quite substantial houses on tree-lined streets with airy wooden porches, ideal for talking and resting on hot summer evenings – districts which would not have been so different from the poorer white areas. So, everyone from the rich land-owning aristocrats to the working-class black felt they had a meaningful place in the metropolis. It was almost like a city of castes, restricting but coherent.

Such abstract notions would have been of little comfort to Buddy Bolden, however. He was spending more and more time living in the fast lane and drinking. Things might have been easier for him if he could have just forgotten about his home and his family, but Bolden was a man with a conscience. And the contradictions in his life were beginning to tear him apart. His sense of guilt at the way he had betrayed his basic Baptist principles was overwhelming. He did not have a clear of idea of what his music meant, and was certainly not equipped to deal with success, much less the sort of adulation he had been receiving. By 1906 Buddy Bolden was experiencing spells of insane delirium, exacerbated by heavy drinking. He often became violent. An attack on his mother-in-law was reported in the *Daily Picayune* on 27 March of that year. During these bouts of illness he could not play and by returning home he only caused intense distress to his family. From time to time when the symptoms abated, he drifted back to the band. But the bouts of delirium gradually lengthened and it seems that his increasingly erratic behaviour alienated Buddy from his colleagues. Before long someone called Frankie Dusen had taken over the band, which was now a shadow of its former self.

Dusen seems to have been the first in a line of jazz operators who inhabited the twilight world of criminality and prostitution rackets and whose interest in the music was, to put it mildly, marginal. Bolden's repertory was never sexually meek, but Dusen emphasized the raunchy elements at the expense of everything else. The earthy vigour of Bolden gave way to the sullen male ambience of cheap pornography. During this time, Buddy was becoming estranged from both his band and his family. His final engagement, in 1906, was not as a band leader but as a sideman. He was working with Henry Allen Senior's Brass Band, who had been booked to mark Labour Day with a street parade. Early September generally sees little relief from the fierce summer heat in New Orleans and this year was no exception. As the band got ready to march the weather was humid and enervating. Bolden set off in line, seemingly without any problems, but he was carrying with him his heavy load of anxieties, grievances and guilt.

Having been fired from his own band, King Bolden was reduced to being a sideman with an outfit that knew little of jazz or of his recent renown. Their music seemed to him as stifling as the weather. What is more, habitual heavy drinking had weakened Buddy's grasp on reality. Suddenly, he cracked. His playing, increasingly erratic and manic, finally descended into incoherent dissonance. Before long he lost step as well and wandered off, still playing, into the side streets. The parade moved on without him. He was lost in his own world and obsessed by a tune that no-one else could understand. Buddy Bolden never completed this final engagement.

Shortly after this, Alice and Cora Bolden decided that enough was enough and that Buddy had to be confined because he was becoming a danger to himself and to others. He was collected by truck and taken to the East Louisiana State Hospital at Jackson. For the final leg

THE DAILY PICAYUNE

TUESDAY, MARCH 27, 1906.

MAULED HIS MOTHER-IN-LAW.

Charles Bolden, a musician, of 2302 First Street, hammered his mother-in-law, Mrs. Ida Beach, in their house yesterday afternoon. It seems that Bolden has been confined to his bed since Saturday, and was violent. Yesterday he believed that his mother-in-law was drugging him, and getting out of bed, he hit the woman on the head with a pitcher and cut her scalp. The wound was not serious. Bolden was placed under a close watch, as the physicians stated that he was liable to harm some one in his condition.

Bolden first came to the notice of the New Orleans press through his misdemeanours, brought on by mental problems. (The papers got the details wrong – his home was at 2309 First Street, not 2302.)

of this journey, over bumpy, dusty tracks, he was transferred to a mule wagon. A medical report on the first King of New Orleans cornet players noted the following sombre facts:

Paranoid delusion, also grandiose. Auditory hallucinations and visual. Talks to self. Much reaction. Picks things off wall. Tears his clothes. Insight and judgment lacking. Health good. Negative blood, looks deteriorated but memory good. Has a string of talk that is incoherent. Hears the voices of people that bothered him before he came here. Diagnosis: Dementia Praecox, paranoid type. [Paranoid Schizophrenic is the term that would be used today.]

Bolden was clearly suffering from severe mental illness which bore little relation to his excessive drinking or whatever psychological guilt he might have felt about his lifestyle. Indeed his manic drinking and womanizing might have been panic reflections to the first signs of his loss of mental powers.

When he was committed to Jackson, Buddy Bolden was twenty-nine years old. The time of his triumph had been brief, a mere five years or so as leader of his own band. He was then destined to endure the last twenty-four years of his life in an asylum. Very little is known about these years. The buildings are still there and still serve as a mental hospital. Their pleasant leafy location in upstate Louisiana seems to belie the sombre and occasionally dramatic events that marked Bolden's last years. His mother's pencilled enquiries about her son's health received replies like this: 'He is silly, does no work, and spends most of his time waving his arms about in the air and talking with imaginary voices.' This heartlessness probably caused less distress than the attempts to comfort Mrs Bolden with unctuousness: 'Replying to your letter relative to your son, we are pleased to inform you that he continues to get along nicely. While on the ward he insists on going about touching each post and is not satisfied until he has accomplished this as least once. He causes no trouble and co-operates well.'

Apart from the evidence of such letters, Bolden's years at Jackson were an almost complete blank until quite recently, when a doctor at the hospital with an interest in jazz history started to look into Buddy's case. He tracked down a retired employee of Jackson who had worked as an attendant on the wards in Bolden's time, before graduating to the position of hospital chaplain. Father Sebe Bradham remembered Bolden playing in the hospital band, and that even when he was ill his ability seemed outstanding. The only time he came to life was when he had the chance to play. Sometimes he would become inspired and manic in his playing, strutting across the bandstand in the hospital grounds. 'At times like this,' Bradham said, 'he would play towards the window, or out of the window, pointing his cornet high in the air.'

How poignant that Bolden should recall the scene of his greatest triumph in Johnson Park all those years before, when he played out of the window to 'call his children home'.

Alice Bolden died in 1939 after years of fruitless correspondence about her son's health. Buddy developed heart trouble and died in

Right, the Jackson Asylum,
where Bolden was confined
for the last years of his life.
The buildings still serve as
a mental hospital.
Below, it was only when
participating in concerts given
by the inmates that Bolden
showed any signs of interest
in life.

September of the same year. Cora was just able to bury her brother before she died a month later. Thus ended over twenty years of almost unrelieved suffering for the Bolden family.

During that time jazz had established itself as a vital new musical force. Another New Orleans cornetist, one of prodigious talent, had established himself in Chicago and New York, nudging jazz closer to the mainstream of American commercial life. He became richer and more famous as Bolden declined. In all probability, Buddy Bolden never even heard of Louis Armstrong, whose achievements he had done so much to make possible.

3

Satchmo's smile endeared
him to audiences world-
wide; although the smile may
have seemed disingenuous to
the socially aware, there was
no doubt about Louis's
sincerity.

*Louis Armstrong was one of the most important
figures in twentieth-century music … for
almost single-handedly he remodelled jazz and
as a consequence had a critical effect on the
kinds of music that came out of it: rock and its
variants, the music of television, the movies,
the theatre … Without Armstrong none of this
would be as it is.*

James Lincoln Collier, jazz historian,
in 1974

Satchmo

To anyone growing up in the 1950s or 1960s without any particular interest in jazz history, Louis Armstrong was the aimiable but puzzling figure who toured the world singing popular songs like *Wonderful World* and *Blueberry Hill.* He rolled his eyes and smiled as he sang, without a trace of irony, about Magnolia blossom in the American deep south where picaninnies played in the dust. In the age of forced desegregation and civil rights marches, Armstrong seemed like a living anachronism: a musical embodiment of the scatty black servant Rochester, who appreared in the long-running American television series of the 1950s, *The Jack Benny Programme.*

Jazz musicians and jazz fans who were coming to maturity during and after World War II were puzzled about Armstrong's status as well. When Charles Mingus, the brilliant bassist and composer landed a job in the early 1940s accompanying Louis and Kid Ory, he confessed to friends that he found it difficult to believe that Armstrong was the towering genius that history spoke of. And yet Louis was just that: one of the most revolutionary and creative of jazz musicians, whose most inspired work came in a rush of small group recordings in the late 1920s.

The last forty years of Armstrong's career could be interpreted as a falling off, or even as a betrayal of a huge talent, but that would be to judge his work by standards that were not his own.

Louis Armstrong always gave his date of birth as 4 July, 1900. A resonant date to say the least, and one that is almost certainly untrue. Armstrong came from a poor, illiterate New Orleans family for whom suspicion was the instinctive reaction to any attempt by the city authorities to record details of births or deaths. Unlike the Bolden family, they would try to avoid to any sort of bureaucratic tagging. Among such people it became a sort of tradition, when asked about your date of birth, to plump for Independence Day. And the first year of the new century was as good a date as any. We can never be sure, but various scraps of evidence suggest that Armstrong was born two or three years before the turn of the century, around the same time as fellow New Orleanian, Sidney Bechet.

If New Orleans at this time resembled in some respects a city of castes, where each group had its place, then Armstrong came from a benighted remnant that fell outside the caste system, the untouchables. He was born and raised in the jumble of alleys near Perdido Street where Bolden played in the public halls. There was neither running water, nor adequate sanitation in this neighbourhood of rectangular wooden houses and unpaved streets. In the summer the place was covered in dust, and in the winter it was a sea of churned up mud.

It was a dangerous, tough area with drunkenness, fights and frequent killings. Louis saw more of all this than he might otherwise have done because he was abandoned at birth by both his parents. His father, Willie, went off with another woman, raised another family and was rarely seen again. His mother, Mary Ann, entrusted

Louis with his mother, Mary Ann and his sister. *Right,* the house where Louis Armstrong was born, in an alley off Perdido Street. It was a poor, violent neighbourhood in which Louis was often left to fend for himself.

Louis to her mother, while she went off to find work. There is a considerable mystery surrounding exactly what Mary Ann did at this time, but one theory, which explains a lot about her habits, is that she was working as a prostitute. After all, Perdido Street was an area of informal black whorehouses. Whatever her motives, Mary Ann may have intuited that her lifestyle was hardly conducive to bringing up a child, and so went off on her own to earn money. Indeed, Louis once suggested, in an unguarded moment during an interview, that his mother had been on the game before he was born. If this was true it would explain his father's otherwise out-of-character treatment of Louis and Mary Ann because his second family knew him as a responsible father and husband who held down a good job at a local turpentine factory. It could well be that he took his cue to leave Mary Ann when he began to suspect that Louis was not his own son. Be that as it may, Louis never forgave him his behaviour. As for his mother, despite her obvious shortcomings and long absences, he felt very close to her and believed that she always loved him and did her best for him.

One of the most puzzlingly persistent myths surrounding Armstrong is that as a child, he was looked after by the warm-hearted whores of Storyville, which was the red light district of New Orleans established in 1899 to restrict that particular form of commerce to one area of the city, an area close to that in which Armstrong grew up. This sounds like a highly sentimental way of avoiding the question of whether Mary Ann was a prostitute or not. If there was a warm-hearted whore in Louis's childhood it was his mother, but she was neither ever-present nor a Storyville girl, all of whom were either white or the lightest of mulatto. It is as if out of embarrassment for the family reputation of one of America's greatest musicians, some early commentator had moved Louis sideways about twenty blocks into the lurid world of Storyville itself.

Indeed, the status of this New Orleans red light district in jazz history as a whole is also highly questionable. It is an intriguing thought that foreign sailors visiting Storyville might have been the first people from outside New Orleans to hear jazz music, but the prevalent idea that each brothel had its own jazz band seems almost entirely groundless. Pioneer jazzmen such as Pops Foster have gone on record saying that bands never worked in the district. We can also dismiss the sentimentalized image of a glamorous and exotic Storyville with its sophisticated madames and pretty babies. In reality it was a brutal and venal place trading in under-age sex, with coercion and violence the habitual tools of repression.

When he was about nine or ten Louis was back with his mother for a while. She had set up a house on Perdido Street and co-opted the youngster to look after his younger sister while Mary Ann was out and about doing domestic cleaning. The left-overs she sometimes came home with made a pleasant change from the fish-head soup and red beans and rice on which the family had to subsist normally. Louis went barefoot and wore the most incongruous of hand-me-downs – rolled up adult trousers or baggy shorts. Money was very short and from an early age he developed strategies of survival that sometimes included stealing. Indeed, during these years with his mother, Armstrong developed an inner toughness that was to stay with him all his life, however well disguised by the charm and sentimentality which became his hallmark.

One of his money-making schemes was to form a vocal quartet which sang on street corners for pennies. On New Year's Eve 1912, Louis decided to enliven the vocal recital by firing blanks from a pistol borrowed from his mother's boyfriend. The next thing he knew he was marched off to jail, and sentenced to an indefinite stay in the New Orleans Home for Coloured Waifs. That, at least, is how the incident is presented in Armstrong's highly unreliable ghost-written autobiography *Swing That Music*. But since competition for places in the home was intense and given that New Year's Eve was traditionally celebrated in a pretty wild way by all the races, it seems unlikely that Louis was put away for so trivial an offence. It is much more probable that Armstrong had committed other misdemeanours, or was running around unchecked and in danger of becoming criminalized.

Anyway, the stay at the Coloured Waifs Home was real enough and had a seminal influence on Armstrong's development. The correction centre was established by a notable black philanthropist called Joseph Jones, who ran it on a shoestring. He adopted a military regimen reflecting his own earlier career as a soldier, and there was order, regular meals and good hygiene. The boys were taught reading, writing and arithmetic. There was also music: the home had a band which played to raise funds for the institution; it was a brass band of the classic New Orleans type, with a repertory of songs like *Home Sweet Home* and *Swanee River*. The boy musicians were kitted out with smart uniforms. Armstrong was intrigued, joined up and quickly graduated to the bugle on which he started to develop his innate musical gifts. Louis's time in the Waifs' Home Band gave him some rudimentary training in technique and helped him find his way round a melody. This early schooling, however basic, was to leave its mark on Armstrong's subsequent style. He never lost his taste for melody well played, or for sentimental tunes, so that his view of jazz was always coloured by that.

After about two years in the home, Louis was discharged and returned to the chaotic care of his mother. By this time he was about sixteen or seventeen, and the education he had received at the home would have to suffice, because further schooling was not on the family's agenda. He needed to work to help with his mother's finances, so he got a job delivering coal for a company called C. A. Andrews. Driving a coal cart pulled by a mule, Louis was paid fifteen cents for each load he delivered.

But his musical experience in the Waifs' Home had whetted Louis' appetite, and the miraculous emergence of the butterfly of jazz music from its chrysalis of popular song, blues and African tradition was going on in the streets all around him. Bolden, whom Armstrong had heard as a boy, was already on the wane, but new cornet kings like Freddy Keppard and Buddy Petit were working in the Perdido Street area. Louis managed to scrape together enough cents to buy a battered old cornet, probably one of the many discarded after the Spanish-American War. After his day on the coal cart he would sit in with bands playing the bars and clubs of his district. He was built rather like Bolden: full chested, powerful and relatively short. An easy-going nature and a ready smile made him an attractive and likeable teenager. He also inspired sympathy because of his naive, unguarded manner. When he first started sitting in with bands, he was still wearing short trousers, and it never seemed to occur to him that this might be incongruous.

By the time Louis was playing in the honky tonks and bars of New Orleans, a white band from the city called provocatively The Original Dixieland Jazz Band had travelled to New York to make the first jazz recordings. In fact, they were first known as the Original Dixieland

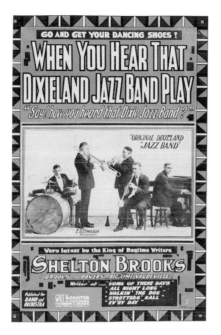

The Original Dixieland Jazz Band recorded the first jazz record in 1917 and publication of sheet music of their numbers helped spread their popularity. They beat the early black bands to the studio because only white bands were deemed worthy of recording.

Jass Band, a name which came from the French verb 'jaser', to gossip, or talk ten to the dozen, a word that seemed to describe the interweaving and busy lines of their music. But 'jassing' also became associated with sexual activity much as linguistic punning did in Elizabethan England. So when the term 'jazz' emerged it already connoted a certain sort of sexual behaviour. The Original Dixieland Jazz Band featured vocalized, vaudevillian cornet playing, interweaving ensembles and catchy rhythms – and it caused a sensation. They specialized in comic 'donkey brays' and chicken cluckings. Things being what they were in 1917, the Original Dixieland Jazz Band had been selected for recording because they were white. Their leader Nick La Rocca, saw an opportunity and seized it. He cannot be blamed for that but later he attacked 'these buzzards who say this music came from Africa – this music is all European in melody and harmonies'. These claims were made in bad faith and can be flatly discounted.

Louis Armstrong would have been psychologically incapable of contradicting such claims, because one of the problems he had in

The avuncular King Oliver
photographed in Chicago,
where Louis Armstrong went
to join him in 1922

making his way in jazz was that he suffered from a crippling shyness
that never left him. He found it profoundly difficult to push himself
forward and always deferred, especially to whites.

The jazz musician who took Louis under his wing and tried to help
the young man overcome his inhibitions was Joe Oliver. A gruff,
imperious-looking man, Oliver resembled a black Eric von Stroheim;
and like Max von Mayerling, the character Von Stroheim played in
Billy Wilder's incomparable 'Sunset Boulevard', Oliver had worked as
a butler, serving in some of the fine mansions on Charles Avenue. He
had succeeded Freddy Keppard and Buddy Petit as New Orleans
cornet king. King Oliver felt drawn to Armstrong just as Armstrong
was drawn to him. Oliver was himself an orphan, and felt protective
towards a teenager who had had to fend for himself from the moment
he first learned to walk. Louis liked the solid reliability of Oliver,
who became a sort of grave patriarch to the teenager. Most musicians
respected Oliver but did not like him, finding the qualities that
Louis so admired merely distant and cold. In any case this relationship
would prove to be one of the key elements in the development of
jazz music.

When the opportunity arose, Oliver gave Louis his first big break.
When the King decided to leave for Chicago, he suggested to his
trombonist Kid Ory, that Louis replace him in the New Orleans band
he left behind. As Oliver put it: 'All he needs is some long pants'.
This was in 1918 when New Orleans musicians were leaving the city in
droves. The great migration of blacks to the industrial cities of the
north had created new markets for the new music, and many southern
blacks looked to the northern states for a fairer social contract. The
economy of New Orleans was also in decline. The cotton crop had
been decimated by the Boll Weevil pest, and the rise of Kansas
City and Chicago as trade centres was relegating New Orleans to
something of a backwater. Storyville had already been closed in 1917,
robbing the city of its spurious image of glamour. For Armstrong,
though, all this was good news, and he took his chance to
play alongside Kid Ory whose band was the best still working in
New Orleans.

Before long Ory was off too, heading for Los Angeles, which he
was to make his base. In California he became the first black player to
record jazz music. The records he made on an obscure west coast label

are known as the Ory Sunshine Cuts. He asked Louis to go with him, but it was much too far and too different for the timid and provincial Armstrong. He stayed put in New Orleans and was once again rescued by the declining economic fortunes of the city to which he was so attached.

The Mississippi river boats which had played an essential part in the United States' transport system in the nineteenth century were losing trade because of the growth in rail freight. The Steckfus family who owned the river boats decided to try and cut their losses by using some of the boats for excursions. To entertain the passengers, they hired a black pianist from St Louis called Fate Marable. Joe Steckfus took a close interest in the music, timing the beat with a stopwatch from his position on the bridge, as he navigated his way up the river.

With the sudden growth of interest in hot music following the recordings of the Original Dixieland Jazz Band in 1917, Marable decided to try a jazz band on the excursion boats. He hired Armstrong early on, and the job was to provide him with the same kind of solid learning experience that he had gained from his stay at the Waifs' Home. Many hours of playing, interpreting parts, and working out counter melodies, helped Louis develop and blossom as a musician. It was pleasant work: as the elegant steamers resembling floating wedding cakes approached the levee of some Mississippi town, the calliope, or steam organ would start playing, to attract the locals to come on board, dance and listen to the music. From Armstrong's point of view, the regular meals and comfortable accommodation were also important. Only the security of this sort of travel could have lured him, very much the prisoner of his own limited culture, away from New Orleans.

As if to demonstrate his reluctance to escape his own background, Louis married a prostitute called Daisy Parker on his return from the river boats in 1921. They met at Gretna, a rough suburb of New Orleans where they were both working. After renting an apartment on Perdido Street they embarked upon a troubled and sometimes violent marriage.

So it was with a mixture of relief and pride that Armstrong received a telegram from King Oliver in the summer of 1922, asking him to come and join his Creole Jazz Band. Louis set off for Chicago with a cornet and a fish sandwich made for him by his mother and

Right, King Oliver's
Sugarfoot Stomp was a
version of his *Dippermouth
Blues*, renamed because he
had copyright problems with
the first number.
Below, Fate Marable's
Riverboat Band
photographed in 1918.
Armstrong is fourth from
the left.

Opposite, the band would
have played on a paddle
steamer such as this. The
steamers made the transition
from carrying cargo to
carrying tourists when the
coming of the railways
changed the transport
system in the USA.

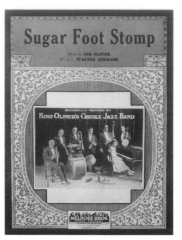

little else except the confidence that the solid Oliver would look after him in the big Windy City. Oliver had a residency at a south side club called Lincoln Gardens which catered for both black and white audiences. It was one of the network of clubs controlled by the criminal gangs who ran the city at the time, and who were in fierce competition with each other.

The band Louis joined became one of the seminal outfits in jazz comprising Oliver and Armstrong on cornets, Honore Dutry on trombone, Johnny Dodds alternating with Jimmy Noone on clarinet, Baby Dodds on drums and Johnny St Cyr on banjo – New Orleans musicians to a man. The pianist, though, was from Memphis, Tennessee, and was not a man. Lil Hardin had studied composition and piano at Fisk University before coming to Chicago to take her chance in the insecure world of jazz. A sophisticated, intelligent and fine-looking woman, from a middle-class black family, Lil recalled being appalled by Armstrong when he turned up – he was scruffy, fat and intensely provincial.

The residency at Lincoln Gardens was by all accounts astonishingly brilliant. Intellectuals, budding musicians, and people just out for a good night's dancing, joined together in enjoyment of this magnificent band. Luckily we have some idea of what they sounded like because Oliver also made some recordings at the time with Genett Okey and Paramount. It was an ensemble music, with few solos, in which the complex interweaving of the different instrumental voices was like a complex dance. More disciplined than Bolden's band, Oliver's outfit had mastered the same infectious beat, and enjoyed the same collaborative fervour. King Oliver himself had developed the vocalized cornet style inherent in Bolden's approach, turning it into a singing, crying human voice, with animal impressions thrown in. Although there were elements of the vaudevillian comedy of the Original Dixieland Jazz Band in Oliver's playing, it was always serious and heartfelt. His muted solo in *Dippermouth Blues* was certainly the first great jazz solo to be recorded.

Particularly striking on the records are the double breaks where Oliver and Armstrong play together. In the number *Mabel's Dream* Oliver's stately, archaic lead was challenged by the fierce attack of his young protégé. Despite Louis' impeccable restraint, his fiery playing threatens to overwhelm that of his mentor. Oliver was of a generation for whom the recording studio was a troubling novelty, and the great man was probably already having trouble with his teeth and consequently losing power. Why then, did the normally suspicious Oliver invite Armstrong, with his immense potential, to join him? Out of fear, or admiration, or affection or all three feelings? Certainly, there is in Oliver's playing on these tracks something of an elegiac and regretful surrender before a new and more powerful voice.

Off the bandstand, Lil Hardin had come to recognize that Armstrong's musical promise was matched by well-disguised personal possibilities. But from the start, the interest she took in him seemed to be as much professional as romantic. She relished the challenge of smartening Louis up, she persuaded him to look after his own wages (which Oliver had been holding for him hitherto), she even arranged his divorce from Daisy, thereby preparing the ground for their own marriage. Lil then set about moving Louis out of King Oliver's shadow, where she feared her shy husband might otherwise have languished forever. After a while she managed to convince him it was all right to leave his mentor, but the onerous task of telling Oliver was left to another member of the band: Louis himself was terrified of doing so.

The reason for Lil's intervention was that in 1923 Louis had received an offer from Fletcher Henderson whose band had a residency at the Roseland Ballroom, New York. Henderson, together with his arranger Don Redman, had devised a way of setting brass and reed sections against each other which was to be highly influential in big band jazz. As yet though, Henderson was playing predictable dance music which was 'jazzified' rather than real jazz. The bandleader wanted a 'hot' soloist to cash in on the growing popularity of jazz and he remembered having heard Armstrong in New Orleans. Louis had been playing one of his last gigs in his home town, and Henderson had stumbled upon him during a tour of the south.

Armstrong's time with Henderson was not a particularly happy one, however. For one thing, Lil returned to Chicago to tend her sick mother and Louis felt lonely and insecure. But he did record some fine solos with the band which showed his growing confidence as a musician. A version of the Oliver classic *Dippermouth Blues* retitled *Sugarfoot Stomp* gave Armstrong a chance to demonstrate that he

Following page, King Oliver's Creole Jazz Band, photographed in 1922. From left to right: Honore Dutry (trombone), Baby Dodds (drums), King Oliver and Louis Armstrong (cornets), Lil Hardin (piano), Johnny Dodds (clarinet). For the purposes of this photo, Armstrong has set his cornet to one side and is playing a rarely-used novelty instrument – a slide trumpet.

could outblow his mentor in the famous crying solo. To Oliver's chagrin Fletcher and Louis had a big hit with this number.

The New York recordings from this period which really stand out, however, are Armstrong's sessions with the great blues singer Bessie Smith. Smith was a gargantuan woman who moved through life like a hurricane. Her grave, powerful voice expressed perfectly the anger and regret that fuelled the blues, with singing that was almost super-humanly powerful. The five numbers Louis recorded with her in 1923 are masterpieces, in which his accompaniments are superbly restrained and sensitive. The only other musician present was pianist Fred Longshaw, and the simplicity of the records was one of their great strengths. In *Reckless Blues* Smith's cry of 'Daddy …' was answered by Armstrong's cornet with uncanny verisimilitude. On *St Louis Blues* the majesty of Smith's attack is perfectly matched by Armstrong's austere, sombre accompaniment.

A year later, Armstrong teamed up with the New Orleans pianist and composer Clarence Williams to make some classic recordings with Sidney Bechet, which showed the brilliant clarinet and soprano saxophone specialist at his very best. By 1924, Armstrong had established himself as the foremost New Orleanian, with only Sidney Bechet to challenge him. He felt increasingly constricted by Henderson's arrangements so in November 1925 he quit, heading back to Chicago and Lil.

Louis had scarcely unpacked his suitcase when he went into the Okey Chicago studios for the first of a series of recording sessions which have become known as the Hot Fives and the Hot Sevens. Recorded over four years, these sessions were the most influential in jazz history, with the possible exception of Charlie Parker's Savoy recordings which followed twenty years later. What could be charted in the course of these remarkably fertile years was Armstrong's development from being a leading New Orleans cornet player into a jazz soloist of incomparable power and depth. At the same time, the New Orleans style, which must have been fairly accurately represented by the King Oliver recordings (although these were first cut in Chicago), was changed forever into a jazz of solos and soloists. New Orleans-style jazz would survive in the city itself, and would be revived enthusiastically by Sidney Bechet and others in the 1940s but from this time onwards it became a musical anachronism.

The blues singer Bessie Smith, with whom Louis recorded in New York in 1923

Louis's first Hot Five line-up was still dominated by New Orleanians: Kid Ory and Johnny Dodds on trombone and clarinet, and Johnny St Cyr on banjo. Louis's wife, Lil, was on piano, and there was no drummer. Armstrong's power and melodic invention on *Cornet Chop Suey*, a tribute to the Chinese food he had discovered in Chicago, was played, nevertheless, in the basic New Orleans idiom of a red beans and rice man. But by the time he cut *Big Butter and Eggs Man* the attack was cleaner, the slight hesitancy gone forever. The miraculous way in which Armstrong could play a melody virtually unembellished and yet make it entirely personal was demonstrated by this number.

The early Hot Five sessions also produced the first recorded example of something Louis was to become famous for – scat singing – singing consisting of improvised sounds without words. One of the most celebrated stories in jazz history is that during a number called *Heebie Jeebies*, Louis dropped his music just before his cue for a vocal, and was forced to improvise while recording director Myknee Jones scrabbled to pick up the sheets, and so 'scat' was born. We have the story from both Armstrong and Jones, although it sounds suspiciously 'pat'. Louis' scat singing was highly inventive and showed the same sort of rhythmic poise as his cornet playing. The gravelly tone of his voice was unique and *Heebie Jeebies* became a big hit.

Armstrong saw singing as central to his career from the moment he formed his quartet of street vocalists in New Orleans. For him there was no real distinction between the scat singing which he developed by accident and which was lauded by jazz purists, and the more questionable rendering of popular lyrics, often banal and sentimental, and which made many purists uneasy.

At the time he was making his Hot Five recordings in the late 1920s, Louis was also working as a singer and entertainer at the Sunset Theatre. It was here that his act featured for the first time the eye rolling, silly walks, wild hilarity and self-deprecation that would later come to trouble many of his fans.

Disturbing though these antics seem in retrospect, and to some they were disturbing at the time, they exploited the minstrel tradition that predated jazz. Entertainments put on by slaves for their masters were the origin of this strand of black performance and the genre was remarkably persistent. In its way Armstrong's clowning honoured this tradition.

But there was more to Armstrong's stage antics than pandering
to the racial stereotype purveyed by hundreds of forgotten black
vaudevillians. For like all great performers, Armstrong was projecting
what was at the core of his being – in his case a debilitating shyness.
The shifting eyes, the downward glance, the sideways shuffle, these
traits embodied dramatically Louis' diffidence in a skilful, almost
Chaplinesque way. It was this truth that reached his audiences and
made them respond.

Not that Louis ever showed the slightest scintilla of embarrassment
about the political implications of his stage personality. He loved
entertainment, fun and melody, and had only a limited notion of
what 'jazz' meant in the broader sense. Indeed, he hardly ever used the
word. The same could be said of Duke Ellington and Miles Davis,
both of whom were making a political point about jazz being a white
man's concept, but in Louis' case he eschewed the word out of sheer
innocence. He thought of himself as a musician and entertainer and
that was that. As his stage persona developed, his nickname 'Satchmo'
– from 'satchel mouth' – began to gain currency. It was never a name
used by those close to Louis, but it struck a chord with the wider
public, and stuck.

The 1925 Hot Five line-up:
Armstrong, Johnny St Cyr,
Johnny Dodds, Kid Ory and
Lil Hardin, who by this time
had become Lil Armstrong

By 1927 the Hot Five had been augmented by Baby Dodds on drums and Pete Briggs on tuba. In the group of sessions made by this outfit, solos predominate at the expense of ensembles, a development that roughly coincides with Armstrong's growing preference for the trumpet. This instrument had a brighter, more penetrating sound than the cornet because the two horns had different proportions of straight to flared tubing. As the stately New Orleans ensemble was replaced by solo improvisations, so the reticent cornet was replaced by the more assertive trumpet. Armstrong's *Potato Head Blues* from these sessions demonstrates his instinctive rhythmic brilliance. He seemed able to delay his entrances almost indefinitely, playing against the rhythm relentlessly and yet still swinging fiercely. It resulted in a paradox. Although hot rhythmically, his playing never sounded hurried: it was almost as if he was playing in slow motion, such was his mastery and his feel for the architecture of a solo.

Back with the Hot Five in late 1927, Louis showed a hitherto unsuspected depth of feeling in his solo on *Savoy Blues*. It was probably provoked by the death of his mother, who had followed Louis to Chicago where he had looked after her. Mary Ann's slender hold on life and the sense of desperation that pervaded her every move touched Louis to the core, and he found an outlet for that feeling in his music.

The final group of Hot Fives has a different personnel. Although Zutty Singleton, the drummer, was from New Orleans, the other important newcomers were not, demonstrating Armstrong's broadening vision. Also absent on this group of recordings was Lil Hardin, probably because by this time the marriage was in trouble. Although the pressures she put on Armstrong were highly effective in a professional sense, it was almost inevitable that on a private level they came to irk him, and he felt henpecked. By about 1928 they had ceased to be man and wife and Louis started seeing the much more easy-going Alpha Smith whom he would later marry. The separation with Lil was amicable and it seems likely that from the start the relationship was based more on affection and musical sympathy than deep love. Lil's place at the piano stool was taken by Earl Hines, a hugely talented pianist from Pittsburgh with enormous flair and charisma. The grave duet that Hines and Armstrong put down in this final group of small band recordings, *Weather Bird*, has a melodic subtlety and a quiet dignity that seem far removed indeed from the frenzy of New Orleans jazz. *Muggles* contained a heartfelt tribute to King Oliver, and incidentally was slang for marijuana, which Armstrong smoked every day of his life, but on a controlled almost medicinal basis – one a day for relaxation. In this number Louis reworked Oliver's solo on *Jazzin' Baby's Blues* from the Creole Jazz Band days, with flair and majesty.

The question of where Armstrong's style actually came from is a problematic one. He revered Oliver more as a man than as an instrumentalist and by and large eschewed the more obviously vocalized calls and growls in which his mentor specialized. Louis's attack was sharp and lucid, yet the fire that burned within the notes gave them an unpredictable molten edge that was very exciting.

The magnificent solo on *West End Blues* with its jagged, soaring architecture embodied these qualities, as did the intense and mournful *Tight Like This*. But by the time Armstrong was cutting the final sides of this intensely creative period, Chicago was in the process of being closed down. The gangs had overstepped the mark in their ruthless suppression of enemies, and their easy resort to violence sickened the public and provoked a political clean-up. Kansas City in the plains would eventually replace Chicago as a jazz centre but for the moment the star of New York was rising.

As he travelled east to Manhattan in 1929, Louis was astonished to hear his own records blaring out from open tenement windows and shopfronts. He was probably about thirty-one years old, had established himself as a nationally renowned trumpeter and a cult hero for many blacks. His only rival in the black music field was Duke Ellington. They were, though, very different men who had little or nothing to do with one another, evidence of the diversity of styles and musicians to be found in jazz music.

Returning to New York from Chicago, Louis recorded some more highly successful records with one of the early mixed race bands. A number called *Knockin' a Jug* demonstrated Armstrong's irrepressible melodic inventiveness while his chorus on *I Can't Give You Anything But Love* was played without any changes or embellishments, yet was profoundly original owing to the way Louis weighted and attacked each note.

With the vogue for black entertainment in the 1920s, Broadway

producers were on the look-out for suitable reviews. One of the most
successful, put together by Fats Waller, was called 'Hot Chocolates'.
At some point before it came to Broadway, Louis joined the show, an
event which proved to be a turning point in his career. One of his
tasks was to sing a Waller hit *Ain't Misbehavin'* from the orchestra pit
between acts. Something about the disembodied gravelly voice with
its irresistible good humour and effortless rhythmic felicity struck a
chord with audiences and critics alike. Armstrong's potential as a
major showbiz star was suddenly clear for all to see. At the same time
the white section of the Musician's Union in New York presented
Louis with a watch engraved 'To Louis Armstrong, the world's
greatest cornet player'. The conflict between jazz and showbiz was
born. Not that Louis himself saw it as a conflict. In his mind the only
conflict was between the exploitation of day labour that music had
rescued him from, and fame and wealth. To regard the commercial
route that he embarked upon from 1929 onwards as selling out,
would be to impose upon Armstrong a system of values which he
simply did not espouse. The Hot Fives and Hot Sevens were in this
sense a miraculous accident, created at a moment in jazz history when
musical originality and wide popular appeal were happy bedfellows.
But Armstrong had no sense of himself as an artist, or of jazz as an
art and he would never acquire such a sense.

As commercial imperatives took over there were personal ramifi-
cations, and Armstrong's behaviour in some of these instances *could*
be criticized. For example, faced with a choice between the basically
New Orleanian band that had come with him to New York and
which included his old friend Zutty Singleton, and a lesser more
commercially expedient outfit, Louis dumped the original band with
little ceremony. Singleton was hurt and nursed a grudge about this
incident for the rest of his life.

Louis's introduction to the world of commercial music was by no
means smooth. There followed six years of desperate over work,
nagging personal problems, appalling management, and conflicts
with the Chicago and New York gangs. It all started with Armstrong's
arrest for smoking marijuana while playing in California. After some
initial furore, a suspended sentence was given and Louis went back to
smoking pot almost immediately. More serious was the final break-up
with Lil which had been threatening for some time. Alpha was

By the time this photo was taken in 1936, Louis Armstrong was teamed up with Joe Glazer, a tough manager who master-minded the second phase of Armstrong's career.

pressing Louis to make an honest woman of her, and with the take-over of his career by big-time commercial interests, the final thread of his relationship with Lil, based on her professional acumen was broken, and they parted. Louis gave her the Chicago house they had bought and most of what he had in the bank. They remained good friends until Armstrong's death. Lil never remarried and lived out the rest of her life in Louis' shadow. But it would not be true to say that she never got over him emotionally. She was proud, and rightly so, of the part she had played in making his career as a musician. She deserved much credit for his success, and the memories of the marvellous years from 1923 to 1929 fuelled her for the rest of her life. In 1971, Lil Hardin was playing a memorial concert for Louis in Chicago. In the middle of one of her solos she suffered a massive heart attack, fell off the piano stool and died.

After the initial New York experiment with the mixed small group, Armstrong started to record with big bands. The musicians were generally undistinguished, underpaid and uninterested. A formula that was to remain unchanged for the next decade or so was beginning to make itself felt: opening statement by Armstrong, vocal chorus by Armstrong, final pyrotechnical solo by Armstrong. There was little of the rich improvised melody or profound feeling of the work with the Hot Fives. Some of the material was distinctly uninspiring: one lyric started like this:

Just because my teeth are pearly,
Just because my hair is curly ...

Louis's instrumental mastery was also threatened by a basic flaw in his technique as a brass player which he had picked up back in the Waifs' Home and never put right. Instead of pulling his lips in to address his mouthpiece, he would place it right on the fleshy part of the lip. This caused damage which in its turn caused callousing that made it more and more difficult to play. From about 1930 onwards there was a steady decline in the grace and agility of Armstrong's solos. As if to disguise this he became increasingly addicted to flashy, high note displays. Some audiences loved it, but it was musically banal and formulaic to the point of slavery. He continued to have big hits though, with numbers like *Just a Gigolo* and *Sweethearts on Parade.*

In 1931 Louis made the grave mistake of hiring Johnny Collins as his manager. Collins was a failed mobster with a drink problem who saw Armstrong as a meal ticket. He worked Louis like a pack mule and cheated him out of all the money he could. As a result of Collins' gangland connections, Armstrong's lucrative services became a subject of rivalry between different groups. Many colourful accounts of

Armstrong's connections with the gangs have been offered, none of them consistent with any of the others. It became one of the great myths of jazz that Louis was somehow connected with Al Capone. In fact, the problem with the gangs was entirely of his new manager's making, and the result was that Armstrong spent long periods in the early 1930s away from the danger of Chicago and New York. One trip took him through the southern states and back to New Orleans for the first time since he had left some ten years earlier as an obscure cornet player. He was astonished both by his fame and by the virulence of the residual racism that greeted him there. A radio announcer refused to utter Louis's name on the air at a concert recorded to honour his return home.

Louis's film career got off to an appalling start around this time. In *Rhapsody in Black and Blue* he appeared dressed in a leopard skin. Another film featured Louis conversing with a cartoon character called Betty Boop and then serenading her.

It is ironic and sad that one of the best of Armstrong's big band recordings of this era, a version of *Stardust*, was recorded on the same day that Buddy Bolden died in Jackson State Hospital. Armstrong's emotional and oblique statement of Hoagy Carmichael's haunting melody could almost have been an unconscious tribute to the forgotten first man of jazz.

In 1932, Armstrong sailed on the liner *Majestic* to Europe where news of his imminent arrival was greeted with excitement and enthusiasm. The trip was not a resounding success, partly because Collins had not bothered to make any bookings beyond the opening one at the London Palladium. Neither had he fixed up a hotel, and Armstrong soon discovered that although Europe was widely regarded by American blacks as a haven of good race relations, most London hoteliers would not actually accept blacks as paying guests. When it came to the concert, most of the fans, who tended to take a more purist approach to jazz than many Americans, were puzzled by Armstrong's mugging and jokey antics. They did not know quite what to make of him.

On his return to America, Louis made some recordings with Victor which revealed the true extent of Collins' disgraceful exploitation of his client. In April 1933, he had to cut twenty-three numbers in two days. His lip was infected and bleeding, and towards the end of the second day his upper register sounded choked and thin. He missed high notes, and slid around trying to find them again. A second trip to Europe later that year brought all the problems with Collins to a head. While in London, Louis discovered that his manager, who had promised to deal with Armstrong's taxes and Lil's maintenance, had done neither. Faced with debts and financial chaos, Louis exploded and fired Collins on the spot. There remained some untangling to be done and a few shabby last-ditch attempts by Collins to make a few more bucks out of his hapless client, but basically Armstrong had succeeded in getting Collins off his back. Louis was a good-natured and generous man. This genuine niceness was augmented by a more questionable endemic subservience to whites, whoever they might be and however badly they might behave. But, pushed to breaking point, Armstrong became determined and resolute: his goodwill ultimately was not a bottomless pit of gullibility. After the split in London, Collins trumped his appalling behaviour by leaving England with Armstrong's passport in his pocket.

When he got back to the United States Louis teamed up with the manager who would remain with him for the rest of his career. Joe Glazer was a remarkable man who created an image for himself that seemed to owe a lot to the pacy, low-life thrillers of the American novelist Damyon Runion, and then spent the rest of his life living up to it. He was tough, foul-mouthed and bad tempered. Yet he respected Armstrong and the other black musicians (he would have called them entertainers) whom he represented. Despite the abuses of Collins, Louis trusted Glazer completely from the first day they shook hands on a deal that was to last until Glazer's death thirty years later. And the trust was not misplaced: Glazer was both fair and efficient. He was Jewish, and the relationship he struck up with Armstrong was a good example of the fellow feeling that existed between Jews and blacks from the 1920s through to the 1950s and beyond. Given the assimilation of the Jewish community in America today, it is easy to forget that they, like blacks, were excluded from major academic and government jobs until quite recently. An informal alliance grew up, whereby Jewish managers represented black musicians in the centres of power where white showbiz reigned. Glazer, Irving Mills who represented Ellington for many years, and Billy Shaw who did his best for Charlie Parker, were all highly effective managers who changed their clients' professional fortunes beyond recognition.

Glazer bought Collins out and injected some much needed
financial stability into Armstrong's life. From 1935 onwards Louis was
working steadily. He appeared in movies like *Pennies from Heaven,* in
which he co-starred with Bing Crosby and *Going Places* in which he
sang *Jeepers Creepers.* He broadcast regularly on the radio, and the
tours he undertook through the south were helped considerably by Joe
Glazer's unstinting presence, easing the band's way through segregated
towns and cities and making sure they were not cheated.

On one such trip in the late 1930s, Armstrong found himself in
Savannah, Georgia. He had heard a rumour that his New Orleans
mentor King Oliver had been stranded in the town after the collapse
of a tour. Armstrong made efforts and eventually found the great
cornetist, minding a vegetable stall, still neat and outwardly cheerful,
but obviously a shattered man. His teeth had gone, and it was clear to
everyone except him that he would never play again.

Oliver's career had followed a path of unspectacular decline until a
series of desperate and gruelling southern tours, graphically recorded
in a diary of one of his sidemen, the saxophonist Paul Barnes:

*1 November – Having bus trouble. Stay on road all night. Weather
cold. Orchestra make bonfire with bus tire. Get help next morning.
7 November – Bus seized by clothing store, finally redeemed … too late
for Orchestra to make date in Cumberland, Kentucky. Woman proprietor
of Southern Hotel hold King Oliver's trumpet for rent.*

Joe finally ground to a halt in Savannah. He could have made it
home to New Orleans from there, but he chose not to, perhaps
ashamed by his fall from grace. Armstrong was moved by his plight
and gave him all the money he had. Oliver lingered on in Savannah
a little longer, and he must have reflected on the international fame
of the man who had once been his second cornetist and 'only
needed a pair of long pants'. But it was the end of the road for Oliver.
He succumbed to a stroke not long after and was buried in an
unmarked grave.

Glazer had signed up Armstrong with Decca, and the recordings
he made for that label followed the same sort of highly commercial
pattern that he had adopted since 1930. There were, however, some

interesting oddities. Louis, playing with a Hawaian guitar backing on numbers like *On a Coconut Island* was ludicrous schmaltz, and yet the sheer incongruity of the settings provided for some inspired improvisation.

After years of *de facto* marriage, Louis finally sealed the knot with Alpha Smith in 1938. As if the formalizing of this fugitive relationship were destined to undermine it, Louis met up with Lucille Wilson shortly after the ceremony. Although the courtship was to be formal and long drawn out, it was plain that Lucille and Louis would eventually marry and when they did they stayed together happily until the end of his life.

Having established Armstrong's career on a sound commercial basis, Glazer had to adjust to a change in musical taste that swept across America and threatened Louis's continued success. The rise of the swing bands, which started in Kansas City and the south-west, created a vogue which had gripped the country by the late 1930s. Since the beginning of that decade Armstrong had been recording and touring with big bands, and earlier in his career he had worked with Fletcher Henderson. However, this was not so much a preparation as a disadvantage. What the swing bands provided was crisp, sharply articulated ensemble playing of great skill, with the contrapuntal interplay of saxophone and brass creating high drama. Opinions differ about the quality of Armstrong's work in his own band settings, but no one makes high claims for the musicians who backed him. They were assembled haphazardly, under-rehearsed and under-motivated. While they could chug along behind Armstrong, playing mediocre arrangements, they were no match for Count Basie's Band or Benny Goodman's Orchestra, and the glittering musical landscapes they created.

Glazer's response was astute. Intuiting that Armstrong could not compete with the swing bands on their own terms, he steered Louis towards some more jazz-oriented small group recordings in the hope of reviving the public's interest in old jazz. Glazer was not alone in this aim. Sidney Bechet was poised to launch a highly successful latterday career as a jazz revivalist. For Louis, however, the project was not only unappealing but utterly meaningless. As far as he was concerned there was really nothing to revive. He played melodies and entertained, and was happy to do so in whatever context seemed most

appropriate at the time. The idea of returning to archaic jazz forms
held little appeal for him. And although he did what Glazer told him
uncomplainingly, his lack of enthusiasm for the small group format
came over loud and clear in the recordings he made in the late 1930s
and early 1940s. A series of Decca remakes of some Hot Five numbers
sounded dreary and uninspired. A session with Bechet, and the
excellent rhythm section of Zutty Singleton, Luis Russel and Ellington
bassist, Wellman Braud was even worse. Both Armstrong and Bechet
sound choked, probably by mutual envy and suspicion. It was very
different from those vibrant Clarence Williams sessions of fifteen
years earlier.

Apart from Louis's lack of spirit, these recordings demonstrate that
his lip, after years of abuse, hard service and callousing was no longer
capable of executing the sort of fleet, inventive playing that he
achieved in the 1920s. While Armstrong could chug along polishing
melodies in front of a big band, his days of creative music-making
were over. Despite Glazer's best efforts, Louis' career looked to be in
decline by the early 1940s and it was difficult to see how he could
make a major comeback. But in 1942, he at least put his personal life
on a firm footing by marrying Lucille. Alpha was embittered by the
feeling that her marriage had been overshadowed by both Lil Hardin
and Lucille Wilson, but Armstrong's customary generosity meant that
she could leave the scene with some dignity.

The emergence of the be-bop movement after the war only added
to his musical woes. Louis spoke out against what he considered the
arcane harmonies and rhythms of Charlie Parker. But most of all, it
was the militancy and aggression of the be-boppers that offended him.
And the feeling was mutual. Among younger musicians, Armstrong
was known as 'pops' – a term more patronizing than affectionate, and
his Uncle Tom antics (known as 'tomming') were despised. Something
genuine in his personality, however, shone through and rescued him
from universal condemnation. The be-bop trumpeter Dizzy Gillespie
came to interpret Armstrong's antics as a refusal to be cowed by
racism, while the blues singer Billie Holiday put it very succinctly
when she said, 'Pops toms from the heart!' For Armstrong was a genuinely good-natured man, who believed racial harmony was possible
and that, to quote one of the songs he loved to sing, 'when you're
smiling, the whole world smiles with you'. He might have been naive

politically and socially, but he was sincere. Joe Glazer saw this and used to say, 'Forget the goddam musicians, play for the public. Smile goddam it, smile. Give it to them.'

Despite the appeal of be-bop or perhaps because of it, the revivalist movement was gathering strength. A romantic mythology of jazz roots, Storyville, and the river boats was capturing the public's imagination, and in 1946 the film producer Jules Levy announced a major Hollywood project about jazz called 'New Orleans'. Louis, with his experience of movies, was the obvious choice for the original jazzman of all time. A band was put together, a surprisingly good one, including Kid Ory, Barney Bigard from the Ellington outfit and Zutty Singleton. The bassist was, incongruously, Red Callender, a committed modernist who was about to go into a Los Angeles studio with Charlie Parker and record the famous Cool Blues session. In time, Callender would be a mentor to Charles Mingus. Given his musical leanings it would be fascinating to know exactly what Red thought of the movie. When it was released, it featured Bing Crosby and there was a schmaltzy part for the great Billie Holiday as a maid but the publicity seemed to focus on Armstrong and the band he led on camera. So it was as a film star, or Hollywood idol, rather than as a jazz revivalist, that Armstrong launched the final phase of his career.

His All Stars who were to tour the world with him for twenty years

A still from the movie *New Orleans* - a piece of Hollywood hokum made in 1946. Louis appeared as the leader of the New Orleans Seven, a band that included Kid Ory on trombone, Barney Bigard on clarinet, Zutty Singleton on drums and the young Red Callender on bass.

Louis Armstrong on the
set of *High Society* in
1956, with Bing Crosby
and Grace Kelly

were born out of this movie project. Earl Hines joined forces once
again with his old Hot Five colleague, and suddenly traditional jazz
was big business. Armstrong had become an icon, a star beloved of
audiences all over the world, many of whom had only the dimmest
idea of what old jazz really was. The All Stars had a succession of hits,
starting with *Blueberry Hill* and including numbers like *La Vie en rose*

and *C'est si bon*. In interviews, Louis sentimentalized his childhood in New Orleans. He seemed to be proffering his own version of the American dream, one that included even the poorest of blacks. Perhaps that is why he was loved so much. In 1952 a *Downbeat Magazine* poll voted him the most important musical figure of all time. Duke Ellington was placed second, and J. S. Bach seventh. Louis had become the world's favourite and most sweet tempered black man.

All this was rudely interrupted in 1957. School segregation had been banned, and blacks in the south were beginning to insist on their rights. The most notorious test case was in Little Rock, Arkansas, where the Governor, Orville Faubus, stirred up whites to resist change with violence if need be. It became a national news story. Louis Armstrong was watching the television in his hotel room in North Dakota and saw the howling white mobs shouting that integration would never taint the face of Arkansas. The incident was to inspire one of Charles Mingus's most famous and militant pieces, *Fables of Faubus*, and for Armstrong too, what he saw on television was intolerable. A young reporter from the local paper, going backstage for a standard celebrity interview after the following night's concert, was amazed to hear Louis use the occasion to denounce angrily President Eisenhower's policy on race as gutless. Before long, Armstrong's protest had hit the wires, and whether as a direct consequence or not, the National Guard was moved into Little Rock to restore order.

Armstrong's stand angered black activists who felt that he should have said and done more earlier, and that he was only speaking out from a position of unassailable international celebrity. It is more likely that the outburst was another manifestation of Armstrong's willingness to be pushed so far, and no further. Just as he finally turned on the unscrupulous Johnny Collins, so he hit out at racial injustice in America when faced with those images from Little Rock – he felt he could take no more. Louis gave his initial comments to a local paper, when he could easily have called a press conference or phoned the *New York Times*. It was evidence of an instinctive response, rather than the politically cynical act of a celebrity.

With racial tensions rising at home, and the Cold War dividing the world, the United States government felt that it was vulnerable on

When black students attempted to attend newly desegregated schools in the south, they met with physical and verbal abuse. Scenes like this one in Arkansas in 1957 finally forced Louis to break his silence on Civil Rights.

racial policy and that the communists might exploit it. They were also concerned about possible communist infiltration of black groups. In an attempt to diffuse international criticism, and to forestall any further outbursts of the Little Rock variety, the State Department hit on the clever idea of making Armstrong an informal roving ambassador, and encouraged him to play concerts in sensitive areas of the world. Louis, partly to hit back at the black militants, jumped at the opportunity, and his concerts in black Africa were particularly successful. Many felt that he allowed himself to be exploited in this way, but it seemed, ultimately, to be what he wanted to do.

On 22 June 1959, Armstrong arrived in Spoleto, Italy, to play at Gian Carlo Menotti's music festival. During the night he suffered a serious heart attack. Fortunately he had a doctor as part of his entourage by this time, who took him immediately to hospital where his condition was stabilized. Against the doctor's advice, Louis discharged himself after just one week, flew back to New York and made a surprise appearance at a jazz jamboree arranged several months earlier. The rest of his life was conducted in the same reckless way. He had to perform, it was his love: it was as if he had to cram as much of it in as he could in the time still available to him.

Musically, Armstrong's concerts had settled into a steady, not to say arthritic routine of love songs and old jazz favourites. On 3 December 1963, Louis and the All Stars, augmented by strings, went into a studio to record the title song for the musical version of Thornton Wilder's play *The Matchmaker* called *Hello Dolly*. When the demo copy was pressed, Joe Glazer played it in his office, and his reaction was typically astute and blunt. He paced the floor, smoking and shouting 'It's a hit, a fucking hit!' Glazer was right. In May 1964, *Hello Dolly* knocked the Beatles' *Can't Buy Me Love* off the number one spot in the billboard chart. The boy from New Orleans' Waifs' Home had become an international celebrity. *Wonderful World* with its ludicrously sanguine but nonetheless compelling lyric, gave him another enormous hit. By this time his trumpet had become a sort of icon, something he held as he sang, like a prop.

It is worth reflecting on the negative way that Armstrong's later popular work has been treated by most jazz critics. Because of their background, such writers generally have a vested interest as presenting jazz as an art form, or as folk art. This approach also helps to justify their own profession. It is not surprising that Armstrong the entertainer scores low marks from these judges who maintain that Louis's pop songs are not jazz. The spectre of the concert hall can be just as destructive to the spirit of jazz as Louis's songs though. It is a different sort of danger but no less real for that. The fact is that Armstrong remained true to his own vision of musical entertainment or minstrelsy for the masses. No one could claim that he was inventive musically in these last years, but perhaps that was no longer the point.

Louis had tried to ignore his heart problem for ten years, but he was forced to acknowledge the precariousness of his health when he woke up one morning to discover that he had swollen up so alarmingly that he could not get his shoes on. He tiptoed back to the doctor and was dispatched immediately to Beth Israel Hospital, New York. Joe Glazer set off from his office to visit Louis as soon as his client's condition had been stabilized. From this point, however, events took a strange turn. As Glazer rode down in his elevator he suffered a massive stroke, and was only found several hours later by the janitor, still going up and down in the lift. He was taken to Beth Israel too, not as a visitor, but as a stroke victim, and one who would

Towards the end of his career, Armstrong was a figure of world stature.

never recover. Moving from ward to ward in his wheelchair Louis visited Glazer and was puzzled and disturbed by the blank oblivion of his manager's features. He had never seen anything like this before and had little idea of what a stroke meant. When Glazer died in June, his firm arranged for independent accountants to assess for Armstrong the current value of his assets, thus ensuring that there were no grounds for suspicion.

Louis was shaken by Glazer's death not least because of his own vulnerability, but he managed to work a little in 1970, even getting to an official seventieth birthday party in Hollywood, hosted by Hoagy Carmichael. His faltering, fragile singing and playing around this time seemed once again magical. It was not the musical magic of the Hot Fives work, but the more visceral magic of a man facing his own mortality.

In 1971 Louis's health declined again. His final engagement, a two week stint at the Waldorf Astoria Hotel in New York that March, was only permitted to go ahead by Dr Schiff under the strict condition that Louis was monitored medically after each show. Armstrong completed the final concert and then checked into the Beth Israil Hospital. His condition was stabilized there for a week or so but he was weak when he returned home to Corona, the suburb of New York where he and Lucille had set up home years before. He was planning yet another concert when he died on 6 July.

Armstrong's funeral was attended by Frank Sinatra, Bing Crosby, Johnny Carson, Mayor John Lindsay and many others. A message was read from President Nixon, praising Louis as an 'architect of an American art form'.

A memorial service followed in New Orleans with the inevitable marching band. Unfortunately, while various conservation bodies were squabbling over how best to preserve the house where Armstrong was born, a developer swept in and bulldozed the whole area. Louis is now commemorated in his home town by a rather undistinguished statue standing in a dull municipal park named after him. It seems inappropriate to the memory of the towering musical genius of his early years, yet it is in some way fitting to a man who longed so modestly for just such civic acknowledgement.

4

A cover design for Sidney
Bechet's accomplished and
literate autobiography,
published in 1960. The title
gives no hint of the violent
side of his character.

*What a moving thing it is to meet this very
black, fat boy with white teeth and that
narrow forehead who is very glad one likes
what he does, but who can say nothing of his
art, save that he follows his own way. His own
way is perhaps the highway the whole world
will swing along tomorrow.*

Ernest Ansermet, conductor and founder
of the Orchestre de la Suisse Romande,
writing in 1919

Sidney Bechet

The clarinettist and soprano saxophonist Sidney Bechet managed to contrive the same sort of vagueness about the exact place and date of his birth as the great Louis Armstrong. We know that the two men were close contemporaries, born just before the turn of the century in New Orleans, but there is no hard evidence of a more precise nature.

Given their outstanding abilities, Bechet and Armstrong should have become the twin pillars of New Orleans jazz – and in a way they did. But with so much at stake on both sides they seemed to circle each other like two wary cats – fascinated but evasive. Except for their formative years in New Orleans, Bechet and Armstrong were seldom in the same place at the same time. Given the definitive nature of Louis' early career, it followed that Bechet was often somewhere obscure when many of the decisive developments of jazz were taking place. A taste for world travel, and a highly developed sense of his musical self-sufficiency made his career both bewilderingly peripheral geographically, and rather lonely musically. His instinctive musical genius and expressiveness, first noted by the conductor Ernest Ansermet in 1919, secured him a seminal place in jazz history no matter how far he wandered from its source. What is more, he could relate closely to a younger generation of musicians, and from the late 1930s until the end of his life he became a patron saint of the Dixieland revival. Mindful of the saying that a prophet is never without honour except in his own country, he spread the revivalist word most effectively in Europe and particularly Paris, where he eventually made his home.

Sidney Bechet grew up in Marais Street in the heart of the French Quarter of New Orleans, with its ornate balconies and hidden courtyards. In his fascinating autobiography *Treat It Gentle*, the most literate and informative of the self-told jazz lives, Bechet claims to have heard Buddy Bolden's *Funky Butt* song drifting through the windows of his bedroom when he was young. His first direct musical experience followed soon after because there was an informal Bechet family band in the house at Marais Street. Sidney's brothers Leonard, Albert, Homer and Joseph played trombone, violin, bass and guitar, respectively, and Sidney himself started on clarinet as soon as he was able, which we may infer was very early indeed.

The Bechets can be considered fortunate in their next door neighbour at this time. Sidney Desvignes was not just tolerant of the noise but an enthusiastic musician himself. So he came visiting with his cornet and joined in the exuberant music-making in the Bechet back yard. It was so exuberant in fact that less tolerant neighbours than Desvignes often felt inclined to call the police and the band would be be temporarily silenced for disturbing the peace. During his turbulent career Bechet was destined to clash with the forces of law and order in more serious ways.

Sidney's mother was an astute business woman and she exploited the talents of the family band in subscription parties that she held in the Marais Street house. For fifty cents guests could listen, dance and eat their fill from 8.00 pm until about 3.00 in the morning. She made about $100 a night.

At the age of about thirteen, Sidney was already showing signs of musical resourcefulness. One evening he turned up at the Twenty-Five Club on Basin Street and was invited to play. He had left his clarinet at home and couldn't be bothered to go and get it. Instead, he picked up a cigar box, fashioned the end into a crude reed and played for several hours without inhibition.

As a teenager Sidney divided his time between orchestra pit work at a theatre in Claybourne Street and playing with the post Bolden trumpet kings – Freddy Keppard and Joe Oliver. After one such session with Oliver, Bechet took Joe for a drink to the scene of his innocent boyhood triumph on the cigar box. On this occasion someone was killed in the Twenty-Five Club and both men gave accounts of what they had witnessed to the police.

It was around this time in 1915, that Oliver offered Bechet more permanent work in his band. The cornet King wanted to add a second clarinettist to his line-up, and thought that Sidney was the ideal man to supplement the skills of Johnny Dodds. Bechet gave it some hard thought but decided to stay with his job in the theatre. It was a seminal moment both in his career and in the history of jazz. Oliver would go on to hire Armstrong and take jazz from New

Orleans to Chicago, while Bechet lingered in the orchestra pit at the
Claybourne Street Theatre. Whether it was evasiveness, or an innate
theatricality in his character that led him to sideline himself from the
mainstream of jazz it is difficult to say. Certainly, there was an
extrovert, flamboyant side to his personality that made theatre work
appealing in itself, for Bechet was not confined to the pit – he often
appeared on stage, swathed in Arabian Nights costumes and
surrounded by sinuous dancers. It was a sort of orientalism inspired in
part by Bechet's own appearance. His light, coffee brown complexion,
high cheekbones and wide-set slanting eyes were striking. He spoke
with a honey-toned voice and natural eloquence that also conveyed a
graciousness all the more impressive for being spontaneous rather
than tutored.

Given the highly conservative taste in jazz that was to characterize
Bechet's later career it is also tempting to see this early preference for
playing in large ensembles as a harbinger of that musical nostalgia.
After all, progressive jazz was created in the early years by the
emergence of the small ensemble from the brass band, and then
by the emergence of the individual instrumental voice from the
small ensemble.

Basin Street, New Orleans,
the location of the Twenty-
Five Club, where Sidney
Bechet and King Oliver
witnessed a murder in 1915

The journey from New Orleans to Chicago became the classic rite
of passage for the Louisiana jazzmen. It was a journey Bechet himself
made in a roundabout way, as part of a theatrical tour with the Bruce
and Bruce Stock Company. But instead of throwing himself into
the vigorous musical scene he found there, he grabbed the chance to
travel to Europe with Will Marion Cook's orchestra. This was a
versatile and spectacular ensemble that featured everything from classics
to cakewalk, taking in comedy routines on the way. So, it was in the
company of this bizarre aggregation that Bechet made his impression
upon the Swiss conductor Ernest Ansermet with 'perfectly formed jazz
solos' before jazz music had truly been assimilated as a form.

At this time, in 1919, the word jazz was often used to mean the sort
of novelty music played by Cook, or the horse-neighing and rooster-
calling cornet and trombone sounds of the Original Dixieland Jazz
Band. It was all the rage in London and when Cook arrived there he
found that even the King wanted to hear it. Thus it was that Sidney
Bechet came to play in Buckingham Palace. Writing of his meeting
with George V in his autobiography he observed 'it was the first time
I ever got to recognize someone from seeing his picture on my
money'. Bechet liked London and when the Will Marion Cook
Orchestra continued on their tour he stayed on, joining Benny
Peyton's band in a residency at the Hammersmith Palais. He was also
giving music lessons to help finance his stay. Bechet had an enquiring
mind and teaching came naturally to him. Some research he was
doing on his own behalf in London turned up an obscure record by
a group called the Six Brown Brothers, which was to be highly
influential on his development.

The Six Brown Brothers played the six instruments of the
saxophone family from bass, right up to the tiny sopranini, as a sort
of vaudeville act. It was the soprano sax that caught Bechet's
attention. He experimented with the instrument and found that it
could cope with the extraordinary power of his playing better than
the clarinet, and its range was similar. He particularly enjoyed the
rapid vibrato that the instrument was capable of producing. No one
had ever thought of using the soprano sax as a solo instrument before,
and as if to emphasise the originality of the idea, Sidney eschewed
the conventional down-turned configuration with a bell at the end
and went for a brand new, straightened-out model.

Benny Peyton's Band, photographed in London in 1920. Sidney Bechet is sitting far right, in oriental garb.

Bechet's musical expressiveness and eloquence was one side of his personality. He also had a fierce temper and loved to drink. He was never an habitual drinker in the way that Bolden was. His drinking came in fits and spurts, and the effect on his behaviour was unpredictable. There was a vicious, paranoid and violent streak in Bechet's character, and a skinful of alcohol brought it out. It was almost as if he had Jekyll and Hyde sides to his personality, and this haunted him all his life. It first got him into serious trouble during his stay in London. Out on the town with a piano player called George Clapham, Bechet picked up, in his own words, 'a couple of tarts'. What exactly Bechet's plans were for the evening we can only speculate, but in any case the girls did not co-operate and he did not get what he wanted. His reaction was not in the least bit gentlemanly and he hit out at one of the women. The police became involved and Bechet was charged. After brief sojourns in Pentonville and Brixton, he was deported to

New York. Some years later the case was reviewed and it was then
concluded that the offence was after all a trivial one and Bechet was
of basic good character and free to return to England whenever
he wished.

The judgement would have been a relief to Sidney, because Europe
had made a powerful impression on him, despite his misdemeanours.
Europeans seemed to appreciate jazz-type music unencumbered by
the historical baggage of slavery, emancipation and reconstruction.
He had played, with Will Marion Cook, in symphony halls to polite,
quiet but appreciative audiences and this appealed to Bechet's burgeoning sense of himself as an artist. The lure of the symphony hall
hangs over jazz almost ominously, a sort of emasculating musical
version of the clown's wish to play Hamlet. This was not the case for
Bechet, however, who had a unique place in the hearts and minds
of a wide range of European music lovers.

When he got back to New York courtesy of the British authorities,
Bechet discovered that the New Orleans diaspora was already there.
Before long he met up with the pianist, Clarence Williams, an old
friend from his Marais Street days. Williams was full of the news that
record companies were occasionally willing to record black bands
and invited Bechet to cut his first disc with him. On *Wildcat Blues*
Sidney's soprano saxophone soars above the static with an almost
awesome vigour. Thomas Morris, the trumpeter on the session was
virtually eclipsed by the power and inventiveness of Bechet's playing.
The 'B' side of the record is no less remarkable. In *Kansas City Man
Blues* Sidney produces a series of astonishing choruses that despite
their unmistakable New Orleans roots, have a melodic inventiveness
that anticipates Charlie Parker.

Bechet's first recording predated the great Hot Five session of
Louis Armstrong, and its importance in the history of jazz has been
underrated, partly because of the primitive acoustic methods of
recording which made listening such hard work. The earliest innovations in jazz are generally considered to have come through the
line of New Orleans trumpet kings – Bolden, Keppard, Oliver and
Armstrong – accompanied by less enterprising, conventional
clarinettists, the best known of whom was Johnny Dodds. The
saxophone came into its own with Coleman Hawkins' first blasts on
the tenor around 1929. But this is only a partial truth. On these 1923

recordings Bechet was playing saxophone so powerfully that he not only overwhelmed trumpeter Thomas Morris, but practically blew him out of the recording studio. Not that Morris, it must be said, provided very powerful opposition. The stakes were raised dramatically when Clarence Williams hired Louis Armstrong to play alongside Bechet: here were two instinctive geniuses with bulging egos, formed by the city of New Orleans at almost exactly the same time, and ambitious to become pre-eminent among jazzmen. The meeting promised and threatened much. Bechet was still smarting from having been introduced to Armstrong back in New Orleans as the man whose playing of the obbligato chorus in the famous song, *High Society*, was almost as good as Satchmo's own.

Anyway, in 1924 in New York, they competed gloriously. In *Cake Walking Babies from Home* Bechet and Armstrong swap ever more brilliant instrumental breaks, with an almost gladiatorial fervour. It is thrilling music, every bit as inventive as Armstrong's subsequent Hot Fives and Hot Sevens.

Given the power of his playing and his propensity for getting into trouble, it was not surprising that Sidney acquired a nickname – Bashet. Sometimes it was used in admiration, at other times almost in fear.

Some claim that Bechet's stay in New York was enlivened (if that is the right word) by an affair with Bessie Smith, the powerful blues singer with a daunting reputation for hard living and loving. Even the tireless Bechet may have been intimidated by this rabelaisian woman, because before long he was off again to Europe. He was travelling with the *Revue negre* starring Josephine Baker and the destination was Paris, where the band had been booked into the Champs Elysée Theatre. The show then travelled to Brussels and Berlin, where Bechet ran into Benny Peyton again. Peyton had set up a trip to Russia and needless to say Bechet was attracted by the idea: Moscow, Karkov, Kiev and Odessa were on the itinerary; it did not take Sidney long to talk his way into the line-up.

After all, there was Russian vodka to be sampled, and sample it Bechet did, with enthusiastic determination. Indeed, his taste for the spirit led to a minor consular incident. According to his own account, Sidney got fired up on the best quality stuff and, overwhelmed by the beauty of the Russian winter, took a walk in the snow forgetting his

Opposite, the great singer and entertainer Josephine Baker, with whom Sidney Bechet worked in the late 1920s. She specialized in mildly sexy skits, miming instruments and doing funny dances with members of the band.

overcoat and hat. He came down with 'flu and had to delay his departure, and his visa had to be extended. But colleagues said more
prosaically that Bechet simply had a colossal hangover and missed the
train. There was a sort of Chekhovian poetry about Sidney's version
of events, which was consistent with the highly creative approach he
took when it came to interpreting the events of his life.

Incongruous though it is to think of American big bands criss-
crossing Russia while Stalin was conducting his horrific purges,
Peyton's men ran into Sam Wooding, who was touring the country at
the same time. He had hired the New Orleans musician Tommy
Ladnier to lead the trumpet section of his band. It is typical of the
exotic contours of Bechet's career and its paradoxes of rootedness and
restlessness, that he should meet Tommy, a fellow New Orleanian, for
the first time in Russia; he was a musician who was to play an
important part in Bechet's career as a Dixieland revivalist later in
the 1930s.

After the Peyton tour, Sidney displayed his usual knack for finding
work and also having a good time. Dodging between Moscow, Berlin
and Paris, he eventually ended up in Noble Sissle's Orchestra, which
was holding down a successful residency in the French capital. But the
Dr Hyde side of Bechet's personality was about to reassert itself, with
more serious consequences this time. Sidney was drinking with a
bunch of musicians in Bricktops Club when a row broke out over who
should buy the next round. A disaffected group including guitarist
Mike McKendrick and pianist Glover Compton, feeling that it was
Bechet who had the honour, left in a huff and went to another bar.
Glover Compton remembered the incident like this:

*Sidney evidently went and got a revolver, Mike had one in his pocket.
And anyway, Sidney passes the Costa Bar and looked in there for Mike.
Mike stepped out on the sidewalk and I stepped out right behind Mike.
And when I stepped out that's when the shooting started. And the first shot
got me right through the leg right up to the knee.*

Two innocent onlookers were also wounded, although Bechet and
McKendrick were unscathed. Both men were sent down for fifteen
months. They were released after about a year for good behaviour, but
the trauma had turned Bechet's hair grey. Although he was still in his

mid-thirties, he suddenly had the appearance of a grave patriarch. It was something he would exploit very cleverly before too long.

After his prison sentence, Bechet worked for a while in Berlin and Holland to scrape together the money to get back to America, and taking the boat to New York, he hoped to put the Paris incident well and truly behind him. He was delighted to find that Noble Sissle's Band had also left Europe and were playing in Manhattan. What is more, his new-found Russian comrade Tommy Ladnier had joined Sissle's outfit. Before long Bechet was back in the saxophone section, doubling on baritone and soprano. However, the music was very formal and rather pallid, and pretty soon the bored duo left to set up on their own.

It was 1932 and the swing bands were beginning to produce a sophisticated, exciting sound that was taking jazz into new territory. Bechet and Ladnier's response to this development was to invoke their origins and the origins of the music in a self-conscious and combative way. The group they formed, The New Orleans Feet Warmers, was dedicated to reviving what Bechet considered the authentic and quintessential voice of jazz – the voice of Dixieland. The fiery records produced by the Feet Warmers mark the point in jazz history when the revival movement started in earnest. It was to become Bechet's passion – 'Water is freshest at its source' is how he put it. But since black New Orleans bands were not deemed worthy of recording until they reached Chicago or New York, by which time the music had already changed slightly, Bechet's source was already a little muddied. He also faced the paradox that afflicts revivalists of any art form: revival inevitably means reinterpretation and change, rather than mere re-creation of the original, which is an impossibility. From the start, there was something speculative about Bechet's revival movement.

Bechet's great gift to jazz was to reassert its popular roots as a hot dance music at a time when sophistication was taking it over. The revival also prompted some writers to turn their attention to the subject of the origins of jazz. They travelled to New Orleans and recorded some valuable interviews with old musicians who did not have long to live and whose testimony would otherwise have been lost forever. Bechet's music was highly accessible and therefore injected a necessary degree of commercial viability into the idiom.

A still from the movie *King
of Jazz* starring Paul
Whiteman and his Orchestra.
When it was made in 1930,
Louis Armstrong was too raw
a prospect for Hollywood
and Sidney Bechet was
in Europe. Both felt they
should 'depose' Whiteman.

Sidney's revivalism had an indirect effect on the jazz avant garde
too. It was the pianist Bill Evans who said: 'the person who sees
furthest into the future is the person who sees furthest into the past.'
There were some post be-bop musicians who redefined modernism as
a radical way of relocating jazz roots, in the just the way that Evans
described, and in all probability it was Bechet's interest in the past that
pushed them in that direction. Mingus's ensemble jazz and Ornette
Coleman's free-form solos were both examples of this project. Above
all, John Coltrane's adoption of the soprano saxophone towards the
end of his career was directly inspired by discussions about the
instrument in Sidney Bechet's obituaries.

It was not Bechet's fault that a thousand 'trad bands' should have
proliferated in the pubs and bars of northern Europe. The warmed-
over formulaic music served up by these groups was beautifully
parodied by The Bonzo Dog Doo Dah Band, in a number called *Jazz:
Delicious Hot, Disgusting Cold.* However, given the squalid origins of
jazz it may be unwise to be too hard on this genre, which is obviously
appreciated more in pubs and clubs than it is in books or articles.

Although Bechet enjoyed good personal relations with the
emerging leaders of the modern jazz movement he became something
of a stern ideologist about what constituted genuine jazz. His fervour
about preserving the old music could be interpreted as a psychological
compensation for having been absent when so many crucial early
developments were taking place. Paris, Berlin and Russia had had their
allure, but while Bechet was dodging around, Armstrong was putting
down the Hot Five and Hot Seven recordings that became classics.

In 1932 Bechet's historicist ideas were ahead of their time and the
Feet Warmers were perceived by many as merely old-fashioned.
For a while Bechet and Ladnier dropped out of the music business
altogether and opened a little tailor's shop in Harlem. The room
behind the shop, where Bechet and Ladnier practised and chewed the
fat over a beer, served a similar function to that of Charlie Galloway's
barber shop in turn-of-the-century New Orleans. But as the decade
progressed it became clear that Bechet's hunch was right and the
public began to show an interest in the old jazz.

Sidney's musical brilliance and powerful personality gave authority
to his revivalist stance. He was invited to play with the carousing
guitarist, Eddie Condon, and he used the fashionable vehicle of the

jam session to display his traditionalist talents – there was nothing defensive about Bechet's back-to-basics campaign.

Tommy Ladnier was still on the scene, but his health was declining and with it the quality of his trumpet playing. On the last recordings they made together, Bechet eschewed the soprano saxophone for the clarinet which he played lyrically, almost gently, as if he were mindful of his old friend's waning power.

After Ladnier's death in 1939, Bechet struck up a partnership with a white clarinettist called Mezz Mezzrow; or perhaps it would be more accurate to say Mezzrow struck up a partnership with Bechet.

Mezzrow was a small-time crook who had made a lot of money selling marijuana in Harlem where he habitually enjoyed the thrills of cultural slumming. He was a mediocre musician who moved in on Bechet's career because he saw the financial potential in marketing old jazz. It is difficult to know why Bechet put up with Mezzrow, unless it was because he could rely on him to shoulder the burden of organization, something Bechet had always found tiresome. Then again, he might have enjoyed basking in the obsequious admiration of the young white boy. In any case it is in the Bechet/Mezzrow era that the mannered and phoney aspects of revivalism have their origin. One of their records starts with the following stilted exchange about Tommy Ladnier:

Mezz Mezzrow, low-life enthusiast, drug dealer and clarinettist who befriended Sidney Bechet

Hey Sidney, remember them old blues Tommy used to play?
Mezzrow, how could I ever forget 'em?
Well man, let's make 'em for old Tommy. Hey Jimmy Blake Junior, knock us out an introduction on the piano and take it away.

It is worth remembering that Ladnier was a musician who made little impact in his native New Orleans or in Chicago or New York in the 1920s. The man celebrated in this song as possessing almost primeval jazz authenticity in reality owed his fame almost entirely to the revival movement, which in turn, had its seeds in Ladnier's meeting with Bechet in Russia around 1930.

Sidney was milking the revival for all it was worth. Still in his forties, he was only too pleased when his head of grey hair led people to assume that he was much older. Indeed, it is possible that the mystery about Bechet's date of birth may be obfuscation, dating from

around the time of this revivalist boom. In 1940 he got back together
with his old bugbear Louis Armstrong, and so disappointing were
their recordings that it is difficult to avoid the conclusion that both
men were too wary of their reputations to play the relaxed, powerful
jazz they were really capable of.

The revivalist movement was throwing up some truly hoary relics
of the old era. Bunk Johnson, a New Orleans cornetist of great
antiquity was rediscovered and after extensive remedial dental work,
even started playing again. Bechet was not slow teaming up with
Bunk, and was even photographed with him 'way down yonder in
New Orleans' where history seemed to be rewriting itself. Bunk
himself had moved in on the nostalgia market, with voluminous
reminiscences of the Bolden era. It is difficult to assess the veracity of
his claims about the early days of jazz. Much of what he said about
Bolden (that he was a barber and edited a scandal sheet for example)
has been roundly refuted by subsequent scholarship and it is difficult
to avoid the conclusion that Bunk was at times a little 'generous' with
the truth.

On the bandstand Bunk's idea of being a 'primitive' often seemed
to be limited to playing the wrong notes. Bechet lost his patience
with Bunk about this, as was witnessed by the critic Nat Hentoff in a
club they played in Boston. Bechet had spoken to Bunk on several
occasions about the mistakes he was making but Bunk carried on in
his own sweet way, so Sidney decided to give the ageing trumpeter a
message he could not ignore. During Bunk's next solo, Bechet went
down to the bar and ordered ten glasses of brandy. Every time he
heard a mistake Sidney drank off a glass and then threw it perilously
close to Bunk's head. As Hentoff put it, 'Sidney was making
his points.'

Sidney Bechet at the height
of his revivalist phase,
playing at the Savoy Club in
Boston in the 1940s

When it came to recording, Bechet could pick and choose the best
of the traditional revival trumpeters. The two he most liked working
with in the 1940s were Mugsy Spanier and Wild Bill Davison, each of
whom developed different ways of coping with Bechet's unparalleled
power. Both were well equipped to do so as they were strong horn
players in their own right. In Wild Bill's case, the music making was
enhanced by the close friendship that developed between the two
men. Sidney took the trumpeter to his favourite haunts in Harlem,
Chicago south-side and the black quarter of Washington. Bechet's

Sidney Bechet, second from right, playing with Bunk Johnson on cornet at Jimmy Ryan's Club in New York in 1945; although Bechet appreciated Bunk's authenticity, the cornet player's inaccuracy was a bone of contention between the two men.

innate graciousness was always evident, except when the Mr Hyde aspect of his personality suddenly flared up. Davison witnessed a pre-recording discussion between Sidney and pianist Joe Sullivan who had a sharp tongue coupled with a disparaging manner. Bechet got so riled by the backchat he was receiving that he pulled a knife on the pianist and threatened, 'One more crack and I'll cut your head off!'

When he was feeling tranquil, however, Bechet could charm anyone, particularly women. He was often to be seen in Jimmy Ryan's New York club in the company of movie stars. It seems that it was not just the jazz historians who were beguiled by the grey hair. Another of Bechet's trumpeters at this time, Max Kaminsky, recalled a particularly startling example of how Bechet's irresistible charm worked. The band had been booked to play an Ivy League party near Philadelphia. The young man who had hired them warned Kaminsky that his mother was a bit strait-laced and did not care for jazz, or the people who played it. He advised the band to give her a wide berth. Kaminsky passed the message on. About half an hour later he saw the dowager perched on Sidney Bechet's knees, laughing and chatting as if they were old friends. Sidney looked up at Kaminsky, with puzzlement written all over his face, 'I thought you said she didn't like us,' he joked.

The idea of teaching, both formally and informally, had always appealed to Bechet. At this time his renown was growing and he felt ready to commission a sign – The Bechet School of Music – which he hung outside his house. One of the first people through his door was an aspiring young saxophonist called Bob Wilbur. Wilbur became a disciple of Bechet's, and moved into his house, where he acted as unofficial musical secretary. In fact, he struck up the same sort of admiring attitude to Bechet that Mezzrow had, but in Wilbur's case it was completely sincere. The two men went on to record together with some success.

Bechet was working on a ballet at this time and one of Wilbur's tasks was to help him write out fair copies of the score. *The Night is a Witch* was a well-crafted piece of conventional orchestral composition, in which Bechet's juxtaposition of strings, woodwind and brass was effectively dramatic.

As the forties progressed the complex harmonies of modern jazz were beginning to catch on, but Bechet's attitude to the movement showed no signs of mellowing. During a gig on 52nd Street in Manhattan his pianist Dick Wellstood played a couple of harmonic modulations behind a Bechet solo that he had been shown by the stride pianist Willie-the-Lion Smith. After the number Sidney turned on Wellstood and snarled 'Don't play them modern changes behind me.' Compared to what Thelonius Monk and Bud Powell were doing just along the street, Wellstood's changes were tradition itself. Surprisingly though, when Bechet actually shared the music stand with Charlie Parker, he enjoyed the experience and even got on well with the *enfant terrible* of the modern movement. This unlikely meeting of minds took place at the Paris Jazz Festival of 1949, when Bechet was still accepting every invitation to Europe that came his way. In London, for instance, the post-war traditionalist jazz revival was under way. Its leading exponents, like Humphrey Lyttleton, were keen to circumvent a Musician's Union ban on all visiting American instrumentalists. Lyttleton invited Bechet to London to feature in a concert he had arranged at the Winter Garden Theatre. The story he told the Union was that Bechet was on holiday and had decided to play on the spur of the moment. For obvious reasons the concert could not be advertised, but word went out on the grapevine that Bechet was going to play, and it was a sell-out. The secrecy of the

Sidney Bechet at the Paris Jazz Festival of 1949 with Russell Moore, the Baroness Pannonica de Koenigswater and the young Miles Davis. The Baroness befriended many jazz musicians and Charlie Parker was to die while resting in her New York apartment.

arrangements only fuelled Bechet's feeling that he was a jazz missionary in a hostile land that needed to see the light.

After the concert he summoned Humph to his dressing room and gave him a detailed account of how he thought each member of the band had played. Bechet thought of himself as the world leader of the revivalist movement and wherever it took root he took it upon himself to encourage and advise. In fact, the idea of overseeing (in a purely artistic sense) the European jazz revival had become so attractive that in 1951 he moved permanently not to London but to Paris, where he had spent a year in jail twenty years before. He easily found his feet there and played with a number of French bands. His most successful collaboration was with Claude Luter, a young man who, like Bob Wilbur and Humphrey Lyttleton before him, was only too pleased to sit at the feet of the great musician.

Sidney Bechet starred in the movie *Blues* produced in Paris in 1955, along with his protégé Claude Luter. They also provided the music.

Bechet's instruction to young players often took the form of quasi-spiritual advice. There was an element of the Zen master about the way he projected himself in these last years. Some of the songs Bechet composed and recorded in Paris became huge hits: *Petit Fleur, Le Marchand de poissons, Dans les Rues d'Antibes.* These numbers tap the innate wistful melancholy of the French popular song tradition and

blend it seamlessly with a jazz attack. Although far removed from the
New Orleans roots that Sidney made so much of, they have a power
and charm of their own. Bechet's heavy soprano sax vibrato even
seemed to have a built-in Gallic throb reminiscent of the singing voice
of artists like Edith Piaf.

The closing years of Bechet's life in Paris were a triumph. Referred
to by the French as their 'Sidney nationale', a statue was erected in his
honour in Antibes. Perhaps the benign ghosts of Sidney's Creole
ancestors were looking after him.

Bechet was not the only black American to benefit from a surprisingly generous French welcome. The influential be-bop drummer
Kenny Clarke had settled in Paris around the same time as Sidney,
and became an enthusiastic Francophile. Writers Richard Wright and
James Baldwin also found sanctuary and respect in France after years
of hassle back in America.

In early 1959 Bechet fell ill with cancer and died in a Paris hospital
on 14 May. He could not have been more than sixty-two years old,
and yet he seemed to have contrived for himself a status of almost
unimaginable antiquity. There was an element of deception in this,
but Bechet's deception was more that of the romantic than of the
fraudster. It was undoubtedly the power of Sidney's romantic
recreation of jazz history, as much as the brilliance of his musicianship, that had such a powerful influence on the music.

5

Duke Ellington's name up
in lights: the Paramount
Theatre, Brooklyn, 1930

*The wit, taste, intelligence and elegance that
Duke Ellington brought to his music have
made him in the eyes of millions of people both
here and abroad, America's foremost composer.
His memory will live for generations to come in
the music with which he embodied his nation.*

Richard M. Nixon, in 1974

The Duke

As we have seen, the myth of jazz roots had gained extraordinary power. Someone like Sidney Bechet could use his New Orleans origins to forge a very successful career as a revivalist despite his long absences from the American jazz scene. Duke Ellington responded to the powerful pull of New Orleans as well. Late in his life he composed his *New Orleans Suite* which included a movement entitled 'Portrait of Sidney Bechet'. Those two words, 'Portrait of' with their implication of distant contemplation, revealed the physical and cultural gap that separated Ellington from New Orleans.

For the Duke, the Crescent city and the deep south of the Mississippi Delta blues singers was a mythic landscape – a landscape as distant and powerful as that of Africa and one that he knew only from books and hearsay. Edward Kennedy Ellington was a product of a particular stratum of black Washington society at the turn of the century. He was an urbanite who distrusted fresh air and stayed out of it all his life; his roots in rural labour were distinctly withered, if not severed.

Washington assumed a special significance for blacks after the emancipation. After all, the government based there had subdued the south in a war fought partly as an anti-slavery crusade. Washington bordered Virginia and the southern states, and yet its District of Columbia status meant that it was separate from them. So the day-to-day racial mixing that characterized the south came naturally to the Washingtonians, but the sense of racial separateness that went with it, did not. There was a sense of pride and optimism among Washington's blacks. Howard University had high academic standards and profited from the excellent feeder schools in the vicinity, the most famous of which was called Dunbar. University graduates could secure good jobs in government service, or as teachers. So successful was the black education system in the city at this time, that when school desegregation was mooted by liberal whites, upper-class blacks opposed the idea for fear that their educational institutions might suffer. The writer Jean Toomer, whose poetic masterpiece *Cane* was destined to be a big success in the 1920s, was a product of this system. The interesting thing about Toomer was that he was of mixed blood and could have passed as white. But at this stage in his life he preferred not to.

The Ellingtons were not from the elite of black Washington society but shared its characteristics of grace and confidence. Edward's father, James Edward, was a sketchily educated man who established himself as a butler for a rich society doctor. His daily contact with wealth and luxury seemed to inculcate his family with a taste for the good things in life. His wife, Daisy, was a genteel, light-skinned woman with a decorous and refined manner. When he was born in 1899, Edward Kennedy Ellington was cocooned in a loving, stable family. His mother, who had lost her first child in infancy, was particularly protective of the young Edward. Her love, and then the memory of it, stayed with him until the end of his life.

The values of the aspiring, middle-class blacks of Washington, DC like the Ellingtons could best be characterized as Victorian. Education, self-help and application were seen as ways of improving one's lot, while in a literal sense, the accoutrements of Victorian England were imported into the sitting rooms of black Washingtonians. The novels of Sir Walter Scott and the plays of Shakespeare were on their shelves, and parlour music and extracts from operettas were frequently played on the piano. The Ellingtons were certainly unaware of the blues or the raw jazz of Buddy Bolden, and had they known about it, they would have despised it as vulgar and demeaning. The sitting room of a middle-class black Washington family could not have been further removed from the world of fetid working men's clubs in New Orleans where the likes of Bolden were plying their trade. Until he reached his mid-teens, Ellington showed little interest in music of any description. Not for him the obsessive precociousness of Charlie Parker or the natural physical gifts of Armstrong. He was a happy boy who enjoyed most things except the piano lessons that his mother made him take when he was seven. He had no patience with reading music, and before long his teacher gave up on him. The first artistic inclination he was to show was for painting. He produced some backdrops for plays at the Howard Theatre and actually won prizes for his design work. He was attending Armstrong Technical School, a vocational establishment which had a strong commercial art department and which went a long way in encouraging the young Ellington's artistic skills. When he later became a composer, his juxtaposition of instrumental tone and colour, and his fondness for evoking places would remain as a legacy of his early interest in the visual arts.

Despite the lack of evidence of academic or musical brilliance, Ellington was already displaying the magnetic personal qualities that were to grace him throughout his life. Polite, cultivated and gracious, he was a proud youth but never arrogant or defensive. He was also exceptionally good looking. By the time he was fifteen or so, the nickname 'Duke', acknowledging his naturally aristocratic demeanor, had already stuck.

Ellington always said that when he did become interested in music, it was for frothy reasons. He was attracted by vivacious company, and he noticed that there was often a pretty woman standing, as he put it, 'somewhere near the bass clef of the piano'. Given the impact that his music made on the twentieth century, such comments have been dismissed as ironic self-deprecation. But it seems likely that Duke meant them perfectly seriously, although like many things he said about music, they were couched in consciously mischievous terms. When he encountered Washington pianists like Harvey Brooks, it was the excitement of the music scene and the image of music making that made him rue, just slightly, the abandoned piano lessons of his childhood.

However, he did learn to find his way round a piano, and although he never quite mastered the technique of separating left and right hand necessary for an accomplished ragtime style, he compensated with quick-wittedness and imagination. In 1917 he even composed his first piece of music, entitled *Soda Fountain Rag*. As he approached the end of his High School career, Duke joined a band run by the Miller brothers who played saxophone, drums and guitar. There was also a trombonist, and according to contemporaries the quintet played a rough and ready sort of ragtime.

In 1919 Ellington took up with a childhood sweetheart called Edna Thompson. They swiftly married and their son, Mercer, was born shortly afterwards. Edna's pregnancy meant that Duke had to abandon High School before graduating, set up home and earn a living. He

started a signwriting business, also undertaking musical jobs in the
evening, both with and without the Miller band. He was gratified to
find that he could get by financially, and amazed that he could
impress musically with a few firmly-struck chords and a lot of
youthful authority.

From the beginning, Ellington teamed up with some of the
musicians who were to play key roles in his great bands. His whole
career was, in a sense, a series of shifting musical alliances of an
extremely intense nature, based sometimes on deep affection,
sometimes on professional respect, occasionally laced with personal
antipathy. Some would last a lifetime, others were short lived, but
epoch-making. Up until the 1940s – a period when his band began to
suffer a high turnover of personnel – Duke always had a strong reason
for hiring someone, and for the musicians he hired, it was never
just a another job. People did not leave easily and when they did it
could make Ellington distraught for weeks.

It was Ellington's natural
elegance – evident in this
1931 photo – that earned
him the nickname 'Duke'

The first of these extraordinary partnerships started when alto-
saxophonist Otto ('Toby') Hardwick drifted into the Miller group
and started playing with Duke. He was from an identical
background, and went to the same school: he was almost family. Next
to appear was trumpeter Arthur Whetsol, a graduate of Howard, and
an accomplished reader of music. Then the ebullient and showy
drummer, Sonny Greer who, fresh from a job with the Fats Waller
Trio, appealed to the Duke with his tales of the music scene in
Harlem. Greer was an unremarkable musician, but he was a soul mate
for Ellington and did much to create the social ambience of the band.

As the various pieces of the embryonic Ellington band began
to fall into place, the leader who emerged was not the Duke, but a
banjoist called Elmer Snowden. A professional musician, Snowden
had been playing for about seven years and had a tendency to lord it
over the younger members of the band. They were not as yet playing
jazz but ragtime hits and waltzes, with lots of sweet melody carried
on alto and trumpet. At this stage, the Duke may have come across a
few tracks of the Original Dixieland Jazz Band, but his experience
of jazz was limited to only that. In this respect, his approach to the
music could be said to have been much like that of most Europeans.
So it was that one of the greatest jazz musicians ever, although a close
contemporary of Bechet and Armstrong, came to jazz in some ways

as an outsider. His finest work was imbued with the romanticism that often comes with distance.

Congenial though Washington was, there was a limited demand for music, and New York beckoned. The vogue for black entertainment really took off in 1921 with the extraordinary Broadway success of *Shuffle Along*, written by Eubie Blake and Noble Sissle, and starring Florence Mills. At the same time the Harlem Renaissance began to make itself felt. This short-lived and intense burst of artistic creativity gave many blacks a sense of real hope and optimism about their future. Poets like James Wheldon Johnson and Langston Hughes and philosophers like W. E. B. Du Bois seemed to be forging a modern consciousness for the black race. Harlem, at the time, was a mixed community with a predominance of blacks. It had fine tree-lined avenues and elegant brownstone houses. Even today the handsome architectural features of lower Harlem can be enjoyed by those who care to venture there. The Harlem Renaissance had an implicit appeal for Ellington, for although he was not an intellectual, and certainly not a poet, in the early twenties Harlem seemed like Mecca.

By 1923, Ellington, Hardwick and Greer were in New York looking for work. Duke met up with Willie-the-Lion Smith, the influential

Lennox Avenue in Lower Harlem, focus of the Harlem Renaissance of the early 1920s. The Renaissance was a spiritual and practical spur to Duke's music making.

stride pianist who helped him form his spikey, idiosyncratic keyboard style. But in other respects, the trip was an unmitigated disaster. Work was not forthcoming for this musically rough, and none-too-original group from Washington, and they were forced to beat a hasty retreat. Back home, the Washingtonians, as they had dubbed themselves, established a regular personnel under Snowden's leadership, Duke on piano, Greer on drums, Hardwick and Whetsol on horns. Another tilt at New York seemed to be turning out as dismally as the first one, when the young men had a change of luck. They ran into an acquaintance they had made back in Washington, Ada Smith, a formidable singer who was destined to become famous as 'Bricktop' – the hostess of a Paris nightclub. Ada was singing at the Harlem spot, Barron's, which was popular with many black intellectuals of the day. She persuaded the proprietor to hire the Washingtonians and here they were plunged into the ferment of the Harlem Renaissance.

It was a good place to meet people with connections in the music business and before long the Washingtonians had secured a more lucrative job downtown, at the Hollywood Inn on Times Square, a club favoured by sophisticates, musicians and gangsters. As Sonny Greer put it, 'the money was flying'. Duke was therefore reasonably financially secure and now sent for Edna to stay with him in an apartment he had rented on Seventh Avenue, although their son Mercer stayed in Washington for the moment, with his grandparents.

Just after the band started at the Hollywood Inn, Arthur Whetsol left, temporarily, to complete his medical studies at Howard. His replacement was a young man whose contribution to the Washingtonians was to be seminal. James 'Bubber' Miley was a moon-faced trumpeter from South Carolina with prominent gold fillings in his teeth that flashed as he spoke. He was a keen student of the New Orleans approach, modelling his style on the vocalized, growling of King Oliver. Bubber was a hot player, and injected some excitement into the rather prim, sweet music the Washingtonians were purveying at this time.

In 1924, the band got a pay rise from the management of the Hollywood Inn. Elmer Snowden chose not to inform his colleagues of this, and to pocket the difference. When they found out, Snowden was ousted and the Duke took over as leader. His natural authority, charm and skill at motivating people made him the obvious choice for the job despite Sonny Greer's greater experience. Greer was not interested in leading the band anyway. The banjo chair was taken over by Freddy Guy, a beacon of sanity and good behaviour in a band that was beginning to be dominated by reckless characters.

Although he was leading the Washingtonians, Duke was struggling to define a meaningful musical approach for the them. They made their first records in June 1926, which are of great interest precisely because they show just how bad the band was. Their syncopated and none-too-accurate music contained little to distinguish it from the work of the hundreds of dance bands around in the 1920s. In *Animal Crackers* and *L'il Farina* Bubber Miley, and a trombonist called Charlie Irvis who had joined at Bubber's instigation, anticipate the growling style that was to make Ellington's name. But in these numbers the technique makes no impact.

In November of the same year, Ellington was to produce his first masterpieces, unveiling an original and fully formed style. What could have happened in the intervening five months to create one of the greatest voices in jazz? Duke himself attributed the change to the influence of Sidney Bechet. The great New Orleanian played with the band for a short stint in 1926, between the June and November recording sessions, so there is no extant aural evidence of his influence. But clearly he and Bubber Miley hit it off, musically at any rate, and between them injected swing into the band. Duke said:

> *Bubber Miley and Bechet used to have cutting contests nightly, and that was a kick. They would play five or six choruses a time, and while one was playing, the other would be backstage taking a nip. They were two very colourful gladiators. Often when Bechet was blowing he would say 'I'm going to call Goola home!' Goola was his dog, a big German Shepherd. Goola wasn't always there but he was calling him anyway with a kind of throaty growl.*

The powerful New Orleans tradition of calling, associated with voodoo and exemplified by Bolden as well as Bechet, came as a revelation to Duke, whose knowledge of jazz was limited to the pallid vaudevillian routines of the Original Dixieland Jazz Band. By the autumn the prickly Bechet had fallen out with Bubber Miley and moved on, but Duke never forgot him. There were two other crucial additions to the band at this time that were to prove more long lasting. Joe Nanton, a West Indian trombonist, had developed a growling tone on his instrument to match Miley's. He was a more creative and original musician than Charlie Irvis, and his unusual technique won him the soubriquet 'Tricky Sam'. The arrival of a baritone saxophone added some breadth to the tonal palette available to Duke. Harry Carney was a solid player, but more importantly, a reliable and easy-going team player, who was to remain in the band for an unbroken stint of forty-seven years. The elements were assembled which would transform the Washingtonians. All that was needed was a catalyst, something to make all these elements cohere.

Ellington seemed to reach some sort of watershed in his own mind when he formalized a business relationship with a music publisher called Irving Mills, whose dapper appearance disguised a Cagney-like ferocity when it came to business. When they shook hands on a deal sometime in mid-1926, Mills forced Ellington to compose so that he could have original material to publish. In those days the real profits lay in publishing, and recordings were seen as being little more than publicity to help sell sheet music. Until he formalized the relationship with Mills, Ellington wrote very little. The great surge of creativity that began in late 1926, must be attributed in part to Mills' purely selfish interest in pushing the dilatory Duke to commit his ideas, however sketchily, to paper.

What was contentious about Mills's approach was that throughout his professional relationship with Ellington, he added his own name to Duke's as a credited composer, thus earning royalties as well as publishing profits. Mills claimed that he virtually co-wrote some of the Ellington masterpieces, and Duke himself never complained about the arrangement. If Mills was pushing his luck in this respect Ellington, an astute man, must have felt he was gaining in some other quarter. What is clear is that the two men had a deep mutual respect for each other. Mills was to Ellington what Glazer was to Armstrong, but because Duke was a much more overtly articulate man, the question of who did what for whom became more difficult to unpick.

In practical terms the 1926 deal with Mills raised Duke above the level of the band pianist who happened to be leader. He became a business partner with Mills, and of necessity, Mills dealt with him,

and not with Greer or Hardwick. Almost by a sleight of hand, Duke
had put himself in an unassailable position as band leader. Naturally,
the other musicians were suspicious of Mills and saw him as a meddler
in what was almost a family, but there was nothing they could do
about it.

Perhaps it was the legal arrangement with Mills that convinced
Ellington that he could and should stamp his personality on the band.
In any case he had done just that by the time they went into the
recording studio in November. From the moment that Bubber Miley's
snarling, whimsical growl announced itself in *East St Louis Toodle-oo* it
was clear that the Ellington style had been formed. The arrangements
were simple, even repetitive, but the whole was imbued with passion
and feeling. What distinguished Ellington's arrangements from
those of Henderson or Whiteman was a sense of intense personal
enjoyment. There was nothing mechanical about it. The fiery
emotion was contained within a strict formality which created a
powerful feeling of pent-up energy.

The dense textural effects that the Duke created at the beginning
of his career were achieved with remarkably slender means. The band
that produced *East St Louis Toodle-oo* was ten in number, only three
more than Louis Armstrong's Hot Seven and yet the deployment of
these forces was infinitely more sophisticated and dramatic. This was
in part because Ellington had a wonderful instinctive gift for giving
his musicians the right material. He did not just think in terms of
instruments, he thought in terms of specific instrumental personalities. Bubber Miley and Joe Nanton excel in *East St Louis Toodle-oo*
for just this reason. As Ellington swelled the band numbers in the
thirties, the way he used different section members to do different
jobs became truly inspired. The actual theme of *East St Louis
Toodle-oo* was Bubber Miley's. It was something he liked to sing to
accompany the words on an advertising hoarding that was to be seen
all over New York at the time. Ellington heard him and used it, and
gave it back to him.

Another outstanding number from this period was *Black and
Tan Fantasy*. The theme, based on a New Orleans funeral dirge, was
suffused with romantic and melancholy feeling for the 'Deep South'.
The structure of *Black and Tan Fantasy*, with its use of march themes
and contrasting blocks of solos, owed something to Jelly Roll Morton's

Dead Man's Blues. The astringent texture achieved in *Black and Tan Fantasy* is partly due to the saxophone voicing that Duke used. There was no tenor horn in the band at this time, and the gap between alto and baritone voices helped create a unique tonal palette. The evocatively entitled *Creole Love Call* was based on King Oliver's number *Camp Meeting Blues,* but Ellington had the brilliant idea of setting the main clarinet melody against scat-sung responses provided by Adelaide Hall, who had sung in *Shuffle Along.* Again he invoked the primitive concept of calling that he had learned from Bechet.

King Oliver sued Ellington for plagiarism over *Creole Love Call,* but lost because his own copyright on *Camp Meeting Blues* was legally insecure. Jelly Roll Morton later attacked Duke for copying his stuff, and although Morton was not to be trusted, the borderline between what Ellington composed and what he borrowed did seem perilously vague. Many of his tunes came from ideas given him by men in the band, *East St Louis Toodle-oo* being a case in point. While Bubber Miley took a relaxed view of such matters it was not always the case. Despite the fact that Duke could often do more with an idea than the musician who gave it to him, there was suspicion and grumbling. Lawrence Brown, a prickly trombone player who was to join Ellington later on, once accused him of being a compiler not a composer, and there is some truth in this allegation. Johnny Hodges had an amusing routine in which he counted out imaginary money as he played one of the tunes he had given Duke, money he had lost by not copyrighting the tune himself. Given all this, Irving Mills' claim that he helped Ellington compose may seem slightly more plausible. Duke's uncomplaining attitude to the Ellington/Mills copyright might have been based on insecurity: if he had borrowed so many ideas he was not really in a position to object to what Mills might claim. Jazz musicians are forever borrowing and reworking tunes, it is part of the nature of jazz but in Ellington's case the problem of plagiarism was accentuated by the fact that he was seen as a composer putting his name on a tune rather than as a jazz improviser.

The leading music venue in Harlem at this time was the Cotton Club on Lennox Avenue and 142nd Street. A whites-only club, it catered for a bewildering mixture of tastes, from the most high-minded intellectual curiosity to cultural slumming to frankly erotic adventurism. As such it became the place to visit for whites who travelled up town with their baggage of confused feelings to enjoy the exotic spectacle of Harlem life. The musicians, of course, entered through the back door.

In the autumn of 1927, the musical residency at the Cotton Club was offered to King Oliver who turned it down because he thought the money was not good enough, which was strange because it was the best-paying club in New York. The luckless and suspicious Oliver thus opened the door to Duke Ellington who auditioned for the job along with six other bands. Duke was late and so was the manager, Owen Madden. Duke's band was the only one he heard and Duke got the job. In this respect he was lucky, but then he genuinely wanted to work at the Cotton Club whereas Oliver's attitude, all too typically, was one of deep suspicion. The residency was to transform Duke from a rising jazz pianist with a few tunes to his name, into a figure of major national importance. Ellington opened at the Cotton Club on 4 December, 1927 and, buoyed up with the prospect of regular and prestigious work, he began to augment his band with some of the great musicians who would help him shape his music over the next ten years.

The great alto and soprano saxophone specialist Johnny Hodges was the first newcomer. A Bechet disciple, he was very much his own man and was to be a major voice in the Ellington band, indeed, a major voice in jazz as a whole. From New Orleans came Barney Bigard with his cultivated and intensely moody clarinet style. Given the amount of material the band had to master each night, Duke's perilously sketchy music reading was a liability. Partly for this reason

Although the Cotton Club was the most famous of the Harlem music venues, there were several others, including Smalls's, where Duke played in the late 1920s and early 30s.

WELCOME HOME THE KING OF JAZZ!!

ALLAN McMILLAN INVITES YOU AND YOUR FRIENDS TO ATTEND

SMALLS'

Gala Celeb Party
7th AVENUE AT 135th STREET

Sunday Nite, July 1st
HARLEM'S HOTTEST JAMBOREE WITH AN OUTSTANDING PARADE OF STAGE, SCREEN AND RADIO PERSONALITIES AND SPORTSMEN

GUESTS OF HONOR

DUKE ELLINGTON
And His FAMOUS ORCHESTRA

RECEPTION COMMITTEE

Bill Robinson, chairman; Edwin Smalls, Jimmie Ash, Gilbert Holland Bessye Bearden, Romeo Doughtry, Billy Rowe, George Rich, Ted Yates, Al Martin, Jimmie Mordecai, Gene Tyler, Allan McMillan, Frank Gibbs, Joe Jordan, Jimmie Davie Johnny Dancer, Rita Munoz, Bob Williams, Willie Bryant, Teddy Hill Lucky Millinder.

BROADCASTING OVER STATION WNEW 11:45 to 12—3:30 to 4 A. M. Nightly
RESERVATIONS: FRANK GIBBS OR ALLAN McMILLAN, EDg. 4-9315 After 9 P. M.

DUKE ELLINGTON

he hired a musically literate trombonist from Puerto Rico called Juan
Tizol. Tizol began to organize the instrumental parts, and even to do
some unacknowledged arranging on Duke's compositions. These were
jazz players of the highest calibre, and most leaders would have been
delighted to land one of them. Ellington managed to hire three
within a few weeks.

There was trouble in the trumpet section, though. Arthur Whetsol
had made a welcome return to the band after completing his medical
studies, but Bubber Miley was becoming increasingly unreliable and
befuddled. Duke was never a disciplinarian, feeling that musical
passion often went hand in hand with personal irresponsibility, but
he had to let Miley go in 1928 when he failed to show up for an
important recording session. A small-scale genius, Miley burnt out
very quickly after Duke fired him, dying of TB in 1932. Then Duke
struck lucky again, managing to poach Cootie Williams from the
Fletcher Henderson band as a replacement. Williams was a versatile
and fluent player who quickly took on the growling Bubber Miley
sound and propelled it into the next phase of Ellington's music. With
the superb line-up he had assembled, Ellington was well equipped
to take on the Cotton Club and to take on the world.

A Freudian would have had a field day analysing some of the
dramatic sketches included in the Cotton Club routine. In one, a
light-skinned negro wearing an aviator's helmet fought his way
through a papier maché jungle festooned with brightly coloured
snakes. He discovered a white woman being held captive by African
natives and rescued her. The two of them then performed a lengthy
erotic dance as the lights turned to gold. It was Mills who saw the
connection between all this hokum and the growling tones that
Ellington was coaxing from his band, and it was Mills who came
up with the brilliant publicity slogan 'jungle music'. Ellington did
not object, and however questionable the slogan may seem today,
the music which inspired it had real integrity. Perhaps it was the
complexity of Duke's own attitudes that saved him from succumbing
to stereotypes. He saw 'jungle music' from the distant perspective
of a refined drawing room in Washington, DC and was as ambivalent
about the whole project as most of the whites in his audience.

In any case Mills' slogan caught on, and very soon the band were
stars. CBS began making live broadcasts from the Cotton Club. This

was at the time when National Radio Networks were being pieced together, and Ellington's fame quickly spread from coast to coast. There was a movie too, called *Black and Tan Fantasy*, which used the 1927 masterpiece as the soundtrack.

During the Cotton Club residency, Duke and Edna decided to part. Duke was an exceedingly good-looking and successful man with a strong interest in women. He confessed as much to his wife – who understandably decided to call it a day. Ellington was an intensely private man, but it seems that the liaisons he enjoyed were honestly and generously entered into: he was the Casanova of jazz to Charlie Parker's Don Juan. Duke never divorced Edna, and consequently was never free to marry anyone else. He provided for Edna for the rest of her life.

To say that jazz and monogamy do not mix would be something of an understatement. A life of late nights, endless travel and considerable public acclaim are not guaranteed to foster a stable home life. But in Ellington's case there were three long-term relationships which he took seriously and kept faith with in his own way. After parting with Edna, he started the second of these: with a Cotton Club dancer called Mildred Dixon. They moved into a fine house Duke had bought on Edgecombe Avenue, in Harlem. This beautiful street of brownstones was known as Sugar Hill and even today it boasts its fine pedigree among the squalor and the housing projects.

Some blacks were disturbed (understandably) by the part Ellington played in the Cotton Club exotica, performed for a white audience, and as if to answer them, Ellington recorded a tribute to Florence Mills, the star of the highly influential Broadway show *Shuffle Along*. *Black Beauty*, which with its quiet dignity and celebratory joy did much to silence the critics. Ellington was never vocal about the race issue, but because of his personal qualities he contrived to give the impression that he was not avoiding it either. He anticipated 1960s fashion by eschewing the word 'jazz' and speaking of negro music.

In 1930 Duke, who was a loyal son as well as an enthusiastic lover, moved his parents and his younger sister Ruth up to New York to live in the Edgecombe Avenue house with him and Mildred. It seemed to work out very well. Duke's father was a willing factotum for the band. His jobs were usually quite menial but on one notable occasion when the regular bassist failed to show up, Duke asked the totally unmusical

J. E. to stand in, which he did, twirling and slapping the bass all evening much to his own and the band's amusement. When it came to Ruth, his sister who was almost twenty years his junior, the solicitude Duke showed for her virtue was extraordinary given his own colourful sex life. He screened her suitors vigorously and if any of them actually succeeded in taking her out, Duke saw to it that a car was waiting to whisk her home at about 10.00 pm. Taken together with the almost pious feeling he had for his mother, this attitude smacks of an almost catholic dislocation between women who are regarded as virtuous and pure, and women who are viewed as temptresses.

In the same year Duke and the band travelled to Los Angeles to make an execrable movie with the black face comedians Amos and Andie, called *Double Check*. The light complexions of Barney Bigard and Juan Tizol presented the producers with what they saw as a major problem because the audience might think the band was mixed. So just to be on the safe side, they blacked up Bigard and Tizol.

By this time Duke was a star. He was invited to give lectures at universities, and to meet the President at the White House. He could play at prestigious venues all around the country and no longer felt so tied to the Cotton Club residency. He also began to feel that the constant demand for dance numbers was constricting. Ellington's ambitions to be thought of as a composer, though vague, had been whetted with the success of moody pieces like *Creole Love Call*. Simultaneously, the management of the Cotton Club was showing an interest in a flamboyant singer and dancer called Cab Calloway whose frantic routines delighted audiences. So Calloway, with his catch-phrase 'hey-de-hey' replaced Ellington at the Cotton Club and also went on to become an international star.

Duke announced his move away from the dance idiom with *Mood Indigo*, a melancholy work that bore a completely accidental resemblance to Ravel. As so often, there was controversy about the origins of the piece. Barney Bigard said the theme was his, and Duke said he wrote it whilst waiting for his dinner because the band was light on material for a recording session the following day. This sort of boastful modesty was very much Ellington's style. *Mood Indigo* was a masterpiece, and we can assume that the shifting orchestral textures that Ellington so skilfully created changed beyond recognition whatever theme Bigard brought to him.

A Cotton Club poster
advertising an Ellington
concert typical of
his residency which began
in 1927. It comprised
Black and Tan Fantasy and
Mood Indigo.
Below, Harlem's Cotton
Club made Duke Ellington's
name, but in the late 1920s
it was a 'whites only' venue.

Opposite, Cotton Club
dancers pulled in the
audiences but their presence
limited Duke's opportunities
to play adventurous or
meditative music.
Ellington's so-called 'jungle
music' was accompanied by
floor shows of bizarre
exoticism.

Building on this, he went on to compose *Creole Rhapsody* in 1931, the first of his truly extended pieces of music. It was widely praised as a breakthrough into symphonic jazz, with Ellington, it was implied, a potential Mozart of American culture. In fact, the development of the material in *Creole Rhapsody* was uninspired and derivative, its bridge passages promised much but led nowhere. What distinguished the piece was its sensuality, harmonic freshness and moody drama. Although *Creole Rhapsody* was successful, it was the inherent interest of the material rather than the way it was organized or developed that gave the piece its power. The extended composition was a temptation for Ellington, a temptation which became more acute when long-playing records replaced 78s.

Duke was also writing some fine songs as a sort of antidote to the extended pieces. The title of one of them became a mantra, chanted by jazz fans whenever they were asked by the uninitiated what the music was all about – 'It don't mean a thing if it ain't got that swing'. After leaving the Cotton Club Ellington had to hire a regular vocalist because house singers were no longer available to him. His taste in this respect was consistently flawed. He invariably went for the trained formal voice that might have sung operetta in the Washington par-lours of his childhood, rather than for blues-influenced jazz singers. He had stumbled on the latter approach with Adelaide Hall's scat responses in *Creole Love Call* four years earlier, but when the time came to engage his own singer he chose not to build on the success of that collaboration. For Louis Armstrong, vocal work was central to his musical creativity and came from the same source as his trumpet playing. But for Ellington, singing and instrumental music seemed to be in different compartments, forever separate. Had he applied the same criterion of formal training to his musicians that he did to his singers, there would have been no place in the band for the instinc-tive skills of Bubber Miley, Cootie Williams, Joe Nanton or Johnny Hodges. Even the most committed Ellington fans often shifted uneasily in their seats when the vocalist stepped up to the micro-phone. But having said that, Duke's first singer, Ivie Anderson, was one of the best, and she had a big hit with *It Don't Mean a Thing*.

Success bred success and the personnel of the band was stable in the early thirties. Toby Hardwick returned to the fold in 1932 after a two-year separation caused by a row with Ellington about reliability.

Juan Tizol was taking more and more responsibility for arranging and scoring, especially on the large number of second rank numbers that the band had to keep pushing out. An important addition at this time was that of a third trombone, to augment Tizol and Nanton. Lawrence Brown was, on the face of it, a strange choice. His smooth as silk sound seemed to be at odds with the astringent tonal textures that pleased Ellington best. It was Mills' suggestion that Brown be hired, and Duke went along with it. His rich, molasses sound certainly contrasted with both Tizol's classical simplicity and Nanton's growl, and he became an important carrier of melody   rather as Hardwick had been in the early days. Brown was a rather grumpy character who was not in the least intimidated by Ellington's reputation. The two men got along badly from day one when Duke introduced himself in the following rather undiplomatic way: 'I never knew you, I never met you, never heard you, but Irving says get you, so that's that.' The first recording to feature Brown's sumptuous tones was of the song *Sophisticated Lady*. Toby Hardwick claimed the plaintive melody was his. Mills hired an excellent lyricist, Mitchel Parish, to put some words to it, and the song became a twentieth-century classic.

In the summer of 1933, inspired or goaded by Armstrong's European trip of the previous year, Irving Mills set up a similar tour for Ellington. This one was better organized and more successful than Armstrong's, and Duke put together a programme which included ambitious pieces like *Mood Indigo* and popular hits, some of which were accompanied by dancing routines. The press interest on both sides of the Atlantic was phenomenal. *Time* magazine dispatched a reporter to accompany the Ellington men on the liner *Olympia*. In England the band was fêted, and at a party given by Lord Beaverbrook, the Prince of Wales famously sat in on the drums.

The tour also had an impact on Ellington himself. For the first time he took notice of the serious interest his music excited. The composer Constant Lambert wrote in *Melody Maker*, 'I know of nothing in Ravel so dexterous in treatment as the varied solos in the middle of the ebullient *Hot and Bothered*, and nothing in Stravinsky more dynamic than the final section.' Lambert's interest gave Ellington a sense of his own potential importance as a composer. Although he had been fêted in America, for him praise somehow had more weight coming from the continent which had bred Mozart, Beethoven and Stravinsky.

Back in the USA, the band continued with its rather relaxed and civilized style of life: travelling the country by train and giving concerts. Mills would hire two pullman cars and a baggage wagon. Duke would have a private room in the first pullman, in which he ate, slept, rested and composed. Old timers like Toby Hardwick and Sonny Greer slightly resented the way that Ellington had begun to distance himself from the other members of the band. The process had in fact begun years before with the formation of the Mills/ Ellington business partnership but had been accelerated by the growing celebrity of the Duke. The situation was not helped by the fact that, because of his fame, Ellington was welcomed at virtually any 'white' hotel in the country, while there was always a scrabble to find the other musicians 'black' lodgings.

Ellington loved train journeys. He was fascinated by the sound of the wheels, the piercing cry of the whistle, the screech of brakes. Shortly after his return from Europe he put all his hours of train travel to good use in a sensual piece of programme music called *Daybreak Express* which captures the atmosphere of a train journey at night. *Daybreak Express* also called on the rich mythic significance of the railway in black folklore. It was the route of escape from the rural south to the industrial north; it provided employment, either hard labour on the tracks, or prestigious work as an attendant on the pullman expresses, a coveted position among middle-class blacks; the railways had the power to lift you out of misery, and could also symbolize the drudge of misery itself. Ellington implied all these things in a piece which was without pretension. His most meaningful music was often that in which meaning was not overtly expressed. Two highly successful songs date from the period immediately after the European trip – *Solitude* and *Sentimental Mood*, the second of which also seems to have been given to Ellington by founder Washingtonian Toby Hardwick.

Duke had a way of addressing the piano that belied his relative limitations on the instrument.

By the mid-1930s the swing vogue was beginning to grip America. Although this benefited Ellington by drawing attention to the big band as a medium for purveying jazz, its effects were mostly negative. At its most distinctive, Duke's music employed unusual harmonies and a rich tonal palette; it contained sudden shifts from the contemplative to the active, like those in Bruckner symphonies. It achieved these effects by the brilliant and instinctive use of highly individual soloists. None of these characteristics was consistent with swing music, which employed conventional harmonies, and put crispness and attack before anything else. It seemed that the Ellington mood was in danger of being dispelled by swing.

Around this time, Duke suffered his first major loss from the band. The departure of Miley had been at Ellington's instigation and Cootie Williams turned out to be the perfect replacement. Ellington and Miley had never been close personally but Arthur Whetsol was one of Duke's oldest friends and a thoroughly admirable man. Not a great soloist, Whetsol was typical of those band members whose limited talents were brilliantly exploited by Ellington. So it was with great sadness that Duke learned that Whetsol was seriously ill with a brain tumour and would have to leave. He was replaced in the band by the excellent Rex Stewart, but he could never be replaced in the Duke's affections. Whetsol died a few years later.

The biggest emotional bombshell to hit Ellington was the death of his beloved mother, Daisy, from cancer in 1935. He spent the last three days of her life with his head next to hers on her pillow. After, he was devastated for weeks, and depressed for months. Duke's father survived his wife by two years before he too passed on. The only family member left to Ellington was his much loved sister, Ruth.

The musical tribute that Duke paid to his mother was his third extended piece *Reminiscing in Tempo*. It was this work which revealed the limitations in Ellington's compositional technique. It was only twelve minutes long but seemed much longer simply because it lacked variety and contrast. Like his other long pieces it always seemed to be on the point of arriving at some major musical declaration and yet never quite did so. Ellington's grasp of compositional technique was sketchy indeed, and at this stage in his career he was not going to ask anyone for advice. He showed enthusiasm when introduced to the works of Stravinsky, but in truth he rarely listened to classical music of his own volition. The notion of Ellington as a composer in the classical sense is something of a myth, and a misleading one at that.

Given a place, a mood and an appropriate instrumental voice, however, Ellington was without rival. For example, the *Clarinet*

Igor Stravinsky photographed at his piano in Paris in 1934. His music appealed to Ellington, and jazz appealed to Stravinsky, but the similarities between their work have been greatly exaggerated.

Lament of this period, featuring Barney Bigard, evoked the rich beauty of the Creole world in New Orleans, with passion and nostalgia – and all in three minutes. Similarly, in a number issued as *Echoes of Harlem*, with Cootie Williams on trumpet, he revived the jungle sounds of the 1920s. The old Cotton Club had closed down because of a major race riot in Harlem, the piece captures a sense of loss and sadness.

The new Cotton Club was located in midtown Manhattan, and the band was playing there when Duke met Beatrice Ellis, the woman with whom he was to form the third and final long-term relationship of his life. Mildred, sensing that Beatrice was 'different from the others' moved away from Ellington and New York. Duke sold the Edgecombe Avenue house and bought an apartment in St Nicholas Avenue, where he was to live with Beatrice until the end of his life.

Like his fellow big band leaders Count Basie and Benny Goodman, Ellington masterminded a series of small group recordings drawing on the talents of his leading sidemen. Hodges, Bigard and Williams were particularly prominent. These late 1930s pieces were of the highest calibre; Hodges's *Jeeps Blues* and Bigard's *Clouds in my Heart* were outstanding. They are suffused with an Ellingtonian spirit and Duke plays piano on all of them, revealing his tact and skill as a rhythm section pianist. Some of the players in these small groups said that there was no one they would rather have playing behind them. Ellington's arrhythmic hints and prompts anticipated to some extent the be-bop piano style of Thelonius Monk and Bud Powell.

Perhaps the best-known Ellington hit of the swing era was *Caravan*, an evocation of Arabia that in some respects resembled film music, once again demonstrating Duke's natural affinity with visualization. The tune was Juan Tizol's. Having fretted about giving Ellington material for years, he sold this one to Irving Mills – for twenty-five dollars outright.

Virtually the last thing Mills did for Ellington was to set up a second European tour in 1939. Once these arrangements were complete, the two men dissolved their business partnership amicably and Mills went his own way. Ellington probably felt that he no longer needed to put up with such a brusque, dominating partner and besides he had been under fire in the black press for going along with the arrangement for so long. The influential Harlem priest and black leader, Adam Clayton Powell, accused Ellington of being a musical sharecropper. However wide of the mark such invective was, it hurt Ellington and pushed him towards the decision to split with Mills. Duke signed on with the William Morris agency and started his own music publishing company, Tempo, which he handed over to his sister Ruth, who ran it with mixed results. So Ellington faced the new decade with a fresh management team.

As if the departure of Mills left Ellington feeling naked, he immediately formed another relationship, one of the most important of his professional life. It was not a business relationship but a musical one. Billy Strayhorn had been studying composition in Pittsburgh, and had developed a taste for classical music, literature and theatre. In 1938 he heard the Ellington band and was stunned. The expressive possibilities of jazz became clear to him and overcoming a natural diffidence, he travelled to New York to introduce himself to Ellington and show him some of his compositions. The Duke immediately took to him, and was impressed by his work. After the band's return from Europe, Strayhorn began to help out in the role of a general assistant. He worked on arrangements, gave Duke tunes, and even organized recording sessions. It was a great tribute to Strayhorn that the hardened old soldiers of the band did not resent this shy bespectacled intellectual in his mid-twenties. In fact, they soon genuinely came to love him. He was articulate, camp, extremely personable and homosexual. Amongst the band he was known affectionately as 'sweetpea', the name of the baby in the Popeye cartoon.

Strayhorn and Duke had great musical and personal sympathy, based on a father and son relationship but Strayhorn, with his superior musical education and intellect was, in one sense at least, the teacher. He pointed out to Ellington how the sort of chromatic experiments he was making resembled the work of Ravel and other composers. Many people had assumed that Duke was already aware of these similarities. One story, in particular, conveys the extent of the two men's musical empathy.

One day Duke called up Strayhorn and asked him for a musical idea to set the first words of the Bible. When Strayhorn called back with his idea, it was identical to what Duke had come up with, except for two minor differences – at least that was Duke's story. A version of the setting cropped up some years later in Ellington's first Sacred Concert.

Around the time that Strayhorn joined the band there were two other important additions. The bassist Jimmy Blanton, with his outstanding melodic gifts and technical mastery, broke new ground with the instrument. He freed the bass from its humdrum rhythm-keeping task by creating a melodic role for the instrument in its own right. According to his colleagues, Blanton's fingers were awe-inspiring – very long, fast and deadly accurate. An unusual mixture of races – half-red indian, half-black – Blanton had an insatiable urge to play and learn, but alas burned himself out very quickly, through sheer overwork.

Given the big band set-up in which he worked, Blanton's influence was destined to be stronger on other bass players than on his Ellington colleagues. A more significant addition for the band was that of a tenor saxophone. The man Ellington chose to fill this spot, which had remained empty for most of the previous twenty years, was Ben Webster. A strong player who had modelled his style on that of Coleman Hawkins, Webster had guested with the orchestra from time to time in the late 1930s. It is easy to see why Ellington felt he needed to add a tenor saxophone voice but arguably, the masterpieces of the 1940s were, as a consequence, less Ellingtonian and more conventional. Something of the exquisite astringency of the early Ellington sound was gone forever with the addition of the dominant middle register horn.

Much of the impetus for the creative outburst that consumed Duke at the beginning of the 1940s came from practical necessity. The American Society of Composer and Publishers was in dispute with the radio networks about the level of payments for broadcasting music. The radio executives decided to try and tough it out, so ASCAP banned all their material from the airwaves. Along with other bandleaders, Duke went into a frantic scrabble to create new numbers for his broadcasts. To be accurate, it was his son Mercer, who had developed into a competent jobbing musician, and Billy Strayhorn who tackled the problem. One of the first things they came up with was a reworked version of *Echoes of Harlem* entitled *Concerto for Cootie*. It displayed Williams' versatility and skill, and provoked a lucrative offer to the trumpeter from Benny Goodman. Williams hesitated, hoping for Duke to dissuade him, Duke did not do so, probably out of misplaced pride, and Cootie departed.

His replacement, Ray Nance, a trumpet player who doubled on violin, was an extravagant showman, but he was no substitute for the solid and honed skills of Cootie. Another blow was the retirement of Jimmy Blanton who managed to hide from everyone the fact that he was seriously ill with tuberculosis. In his place Duke hired a little-known bassist called Junior Raglin. A welter of Ellington numbers followed before the recording ban of 1942 kept Duke and every other musician out of the studios for over a year: *Cotton Tail, Harlem Airshaft*, with its romantic evocation of high-rise living and *Warm Valley*, a voluptuous piece of music, inspired according to Ellington by a hilly landscape which reminded him of a reclining woman. Perhaps the best known of these early forties numbers was the Strayhorn song *Take the 'A' Train*, the title of which gave subway riders appropriate directions for travelling up to Harlem. It became the band's signature tune, and Duke's spikey, idiosyncratic piano introduction was to captivate audiences for years to come.

The recording ban provoked a stampede of departures, which tore the heart out of the Ellington band. Barney Bigard was first to quit; he was tired of constant travelling, especially since the comfortable Pullman train had been replaced by a band bus, driven by Harry Carney. At this time Duke was busying himself with another extended work. His *Black, Brown and Beige Suite* was nothing less than an attempt to portray in music the history of black people in the

Duke studying a score with Billie Strayhorn. When Strayhorn joined Duke in 1939, he arranged Ellington's works for the orchestra, as well as composing in his own right.

United States. The first movement, 'Black', evoked the early days of forced transport from Africa and slavery. 'Brown' told the story of the Civil War, the emancipation and the Spanish/American War, while 'Beige' brought black history up to date by expressing the longing for education and justice, and describing the contribution of blacks to World War II.

This ambitious work was unveiled at a 1943 concert and contained some beautiful music, notably a wonderful work song variation given to Joe Nanton's trombone and the glorious *Come Sunday* section, which Johnny Hodges made his own. However, the term 'suite' as used by Ellington had no technical meaning at all and simply referred to a number of diffuse or unrelated movements put together. Often the structure was governed by historical or literary ideas which were not matched by musical development, and the lyrics were frequently banal. In *Black, Brown and Beige Suite*, Betty Roche sang 'The Blues ain't nothing but a ticket from your loved one to nowhere.' Some of the worst lyrics in Ellington's work were his own.

Black, Brown and Beige Suite made a strong impact, especially among black intellectuals, when it was committed to vinyl in a slightly condensed form after the recording ban. (Indeed, the poet and jazz writer, Amiri Baraka, who used to be known as LeRoi Jones, based the colour scheme of his elegant house in Newark on Duke's *Suite*.) The problem of the work, however, was that it was too literal and the story line seemed to get in the way of the music. Ellington was a poor lyricist and any sort of form which called for verbal exposition immediately presented problems.

In 1943, Ben Webster, Juan Tizol and Rex Stewart left the band in quick succession to be followed by Toby Hardwick who departed for the last time, feeling he had become a fossilized rather than a working musician. Then Joe Nanton, the last of the growl specialists who had helped make Ellington's name in the 1920s, died. Part of the reason for this turnover was that the big band scene was in a state of turmoil. In 1946, no fewer than eight of them broke up because of the changed economic circumstances after World War II. Musicians were no longer willing to play for low wages, board and lodging. Even the great Count Basie band was reduced for a while to a septet. But Ellington kept going, subsidizing the band with his ASCAP fees and royalties.

Throughout this time of change in the 1940s Duke made some

eccentric choices about whom to hire. Jimmy Hamilton was no
match for Barney Bigard and the rather colourless Russell Procope
could not fulfil the very special role that founder Washingtonian
Toby Hardwick had played in the band. Dangerous though it is to
speculate about what might have been, it is hard to avoid the
conclusion that if Duke had approached different musicians to
rebuild his band, he could have re-established himself at the cutting
edge of the post-war big band movement. It seems entirely probable
that the powerful and inventive trumpeters Charlie Shavers and Roy
Eldridge, the lyrical trombonist Dickie Wells, or the brilliant tenor
saxophonist Wardell Gray would have been only too pleased to be
asked. But Duke did not hire players of this calibre, and condemned
himself to a decade of slow decline and marginalization.

The band sounded uninspired and under-rehearsed, Duke himself
looked tired and jaded and by this time his face had become strangely
mask-like, the enormous bags under his eyes bearing witness to
thousands of days on the road and in hotels. Duke's compositions
sounded weary too. His 1947 *Liberia Suite* was written to celebrate the
African state which was established as a home for freed slaves to
return to. It is hard to believe that this portentous and message-laden
work comes from the same hand that penned *Creole Love Call*,
Echoes of Harlem and *Cotton Tail*. The work consisted of an opening
movement entitled *I Like the Sunrise* which was followed by five more
or less unrelated dances. Al Hibbler sang 'Every evening I wish
upon a star that that brand new tomorrow is not very far,' while Ray
Nance's violin part in the third dance is a dismally derivative, pseudo-
Hungarian fling.

After the war, the emergence of be-bop, with its intense, intimate
sound only added to Ellington's difficulties. The big bands that
survived the economic shake-up of 1946 seemed like dinosaurs,
interesting survivors of a past era, but nothing more. Duke never
spoke out against be-bop as Armstrong did, in fact he once half-
jokingly offered Charlie Parker a job. Parker turned him down
because he could not pay enough. The fact that the Ellington band
could not command the fees it once did was one more reason for the
alarming turnover of personnel.

Then in 1951, Duke was faced with a mass defection. Johnny
Hodges decided to call his own bluff and set up the Johnny Hodges

Orchestra. He took Sonny Greer, Lawrence Brown and a tenor player called Al Sears with him. Ellington must have felt that total collapse was staring him in the face at this point, but salvation of a sort was just around the corner. To replace Sears, Duke hired a little-known musician called Paul Gonsalves. Gonsalves could have won a prize for being the most ethnically obscure member of the band, coming as he did from a small mixed-race community indigenous to Massachussets and Rhode Island which had its roots in the Cape Verde Islands. It was with Gonsalves that Duke formed the last of those intense musical alliances that characterized his remarkable career.

As the fifties progressed Ellington managed to staunch the loss of personnel and stabilize the band somewhat. Another important new-comer brought in during the rebuilding process which took place after the Hodges defection was Clarke Terry. A lyrical and cultivated trumpeter from St Louis, he brought a new elegance to the brass section. (As it turned out, the Hodges band was not a great success and in the mid-fifties the chastened altoist rejoined Ellington and just bit his lip whenever he thought about the tunes he had given Duke for nothing.)

Gonsalves was a bit of a mystery to most people in the band. He was a heavy drinker who, if he was not actually playing or drunk, had very little to say for himself. What is more, he had the sort of pallor that indicated he had hardly seen daylight or breathed fresh air. But it was Gonsalves who staged a one-man salvage job on Ellington's reputation at the Newport Jazz Festival of 1956. Duke had premiered a rather sober piece called *The Newport Jazz Festival Suite* which managed to get some members of the audience going – out of the door. Almost out of desperation he called for *Diminuendo and Crescendo in Blue*, a 1930s piece that the band had almost forgotten. He indicated that Gonsalves should solo, but Paul whispered that he did not know the piece. Duke's response was to the point – 'It's just a blues in B flat. I'll bring you in and I'll take you out. Just get out there and blow your tail off.'

And that is just what Gonsalves did. As his solo built, he engulfed the audience with sinuous waves of sound. The drummer Jo Jones was in the front row of the audience and he remembered that by the sixth chorus there were shouts and handclaps. The frail-looking tenor saxophonist was creating formidable swing. Every time he blew, a vein

Right, the Newport Jazz Festival was the most prestigious in the USA during the 1950s and 60s. When Duke Ellington played *Diminuendo and Crescendo in Blue* at the 1956 Festival, his reputation suddenly revived. *Above,* this is the record that was made of the performance.

stood out on his forehead, and threatened to burst. Jones was moved to keep the beat with a rolled-up newspaper on the armrest of his seat. As the solo built, Ellington's face became suffused with amazement and delight. He looked like a man rescued by the cavalry at the last moment. As a public occasion, the Ellington *Diminuendo and Crescendo in Blue* would be spoken of later in the same hushed tones as the Oliver/Armstrong sets at the Lincoln Gardens in Chicago, or the jousting of Charlie Parker and Dizzy Gillespie at the Massey Hall, Toronto in 1953. Magically, Gonsalves' twenty-seven choruses of hot jazz turned it all around for Ellington. There was much discussion of almost theological fervour among jazz scholars about whether the sound of Jones's newspaper beat was audible on the recording that was made of the occasion. Once more Duke was a figure of stature and by this time the longevity of his career was in itself of interest. Gonsalves was not one of the great inventive saxophonists of jazz yet his solo on *Diminuendo and Crescendo in Blue* was more than just rabble-rousing. It was in its way immaculate; a beautifully judged piece of jazz. The whole event was further evidence of Ellington's instinctive genius for using his players in the right context and allowing them to excel.

With the success of the Newport Jazz Festival in 1956 some of Duke's old sidemen began to drift back. Two of his most notable scalps were Cootie Williams and Lawrence Brown. Duke's son,

Mercer, began to manage the band, injecting some much needed discipline into the way things were run. Ellington continued to compose in the last decade of his life, and one of his more interesting efforts was a suite commissioned for the Shakespeare Festival at Stratford, Ontario. *Such Sweet Thunder* evoked various Shakespearean characters with sensitivity and inventiveness, some sections worked better than others, and Duke's portrayal of Puck in *Up and Down* was particularly felicitous.

To Ellington the most important part of his work in this period was the series of Sacred Concerts he wrote. As he grew older, his interest in religion became stronger, and the vague pantheistic feelings of his youth were formalized into more conventional religious belief. Duke's first Sacred Concert was commissioned for the inauguration of the Grace Cathedral in San Francisco in 1965. Ellington was delighted to be involved in such an important ceremony: the sincerity of his religious belief was not in question, but the Concert itself suffered

Ellington's Sacred Concerts were as much about the religiosity of their setting as about serious music making. This one was photographed at Westminster Abbey in 1971.

from the same sort of pretension as the *Liberia Suite* and the libretto was banal. About one third of the music resembled jazz, a third was recititive, and a third choral and solo singing. Too often the spiritual idea of high aspiration was realized musically with one of Cat Anderson's all-too-obvious high-note routines. After a six-note theme written to accompany the opening words of the Bible, Ellington added his own thoughts about the purity of the creation. For him this was embodied in such anachronistic ideas as: 'No aspirin ...' If the intention was to build on the religious feeling of the *Come Sunday* section in *Black, Brown and Beige Suite* there was simply not enough compositional or philosophical scaffolding to sustain it. The effect was of music that was religiose rather than religious.

At about the time of the first Sacred Concert Billy Strayhorn was diagnosed as suffering from cancer. His health declined fast and he died in 1967, leaving Duke more bereft than he had been since the death of his mother. Perhaps some of that feeling went into the second Sacred Concert which contained passages of powerful music, and was first performed at the Cathedral of St John the Divine in New York in 1968.

By this time Ellington was a figure of international fame, and like Armstrong, he undertook a series of international tours that also helped raise his profile at home. He was invited to the White House for the second time in his life in 1969 when President Nixon honoured his seventieth birthday. The President sat graciously at the piano and played *Happy Birthday* for the septuagenarian – who jerked his head in amused musical appreciation.

Ellington suffered another grievous loss in 1970 with the sudden death of Johnny Hodges. The two men had made up after the split of 1951 and become very close. When a colleague approached Duke after the funeral and asked who would replace the great altoist, Duke replied, 'No one, because Johnny is irreplaceable.'

In 1972, Ellington had a standard medical check-up and was diagnosed as having lymphatic cancer. At first he told no one and continued to work at his usual furious pace. The 1973 Sacred Concert at Westminster Abbey in London was overshadowed by the signs that Duke's powers were declining. In January 1974, he collapsed and was taken to Columbia Presbyterian Medical Center for a three-week stay. He was back there again in April, when concerts and recitals all over

Duke sits pensively at the piano towards the end of his life, worn out by travelling and music-making.

the world marked his seventy-fifth birthday. For him, it was a rather sombre affair with a few friends gathered around his bedside.

In May, Paul Gonsalves died in London after a drinking bout. Given his delicate state, Ellington was spared the news of this loss by his friends, so the ending of the last of his great musical friendships was to remain unknown to him because he developed pneumonia and died on 24 May. Within a few weeks, Harry Carney, who had been with Duke for forty-seven uninterrupted years, was also dead. Mercer attempted to take over the direction of the band but demand was not strong and they never worked full-time again. It was all finished.

Duke Ellington was a puzzling, enigmatic man who seemed to be rent with paradoxes. He was proud of his negritude and yet part of him craved white approval. He could be mean with his musicians, and yet after Sonny Greer retired Duke sent the drummer's wages to him every week in a taxi, for old time's sake. He played fast and loose with his own emotional life and yet wanted to keep his sister cocooned like a satin doll. He was a profoundly creative man who had a magpie instinct for collecting other peoples' ideas.

His immense achievements in jazz were built on a surprisingly slender basis. He was a passable pianist who never mastered the technique of composing on paper. He could not develop musical material in a way that sustained a lengthy piece, and for long periods he leaned on Juan Tizol or Billy Strayhorn to arrange for him.

Perhaps the key to understanding Ellington's musical genius is to think of him less as a great composer and more as a great improviser whose main instrument was not the piano but his band and the individual improvisational skills that he nurtured within it. He threw ideas together instinctively with the sounds of his instrumentalists ringing in his ears. He always worked best when he had something concrete to evoke like the train journeys he loved so much or the emotions he felt so deeply. He approached music rather like a painter, the painter he had aspired to be in his teenage years. Because he relied so much on his musicians to realize his ideas, he feared in his darker moments that he was empty, hollow and predatory. This fear was magnificently belied by the way the Ellington stamp transformed everything he was given and distinguished everything he did.

6

Lester Young playing at the
'Jazz at the Philharmonic'
event, organized by Norman
Granz in 1958.

*Pres never played anything that didn't mean
anything. Everything made sense. I don't care
what it was, what the song was, it didn't have
to be exciting but you believe me, if you listen
to it it told a story, beautiful stories.*

Buddy Tait, tenor saxophonist, in 1984

Lester Young

By the mid thirties the success of the swing bands meant that jazz had come as close as it was to get to being absorbed into the mainstream of American popular culture. The precisely arranged ensemble playing, required to make the music of these large outfits coherent, meant that solo space was limited and solos severely constrained. So some gifted players decided to get together in small groups picked from the ranks of the big bands, in order to give themselves more freedom to play solos and experiment. Excellent work came out of the small groups that emerged under Ellington's auspices, and the same thing happened in the Benny Goodman Band and the Count Basie outfit. It was in a Basie small group that Lester Young made his recording debut on tenor saxophone.

Swing orchestras had brought the saxophone to prominence as a jazz instrument. Choirs of reeds were set against brass sections in dramatic contrapuntal arrangements, and the expressive possibilities of the saxophone soon became apparent. In this respect Bechet's career on the soprano was ahead of the general trend. The first tenor saxophonist to stamp his personality on the instrument was Coleman Hawkins, whose rumbustious throaty tone emerged around 1930.

If jazz was progressing, fitfully, from ensemble to solo-dominated music, and solo music was becoming ever more complex and subtle, there was also another dynamic at work. The naive approach of Bolden and Armstrong had been overtaken by Ellington's sophistication, sometimes bordering on affectation. The Duke's jazz was highly self-conscious and along the way he flirted with the concert hall and the cathedral.

There was another way to move jazz into the realm of self-conscious art. It manifested itself as an underground Bohemianism which would always be in conflict with the status quo. This essentially romantic approach was first adopted in the jazz world by Lester Young. His music was even more original than his Byronic stance, although the early years of his life seemed especially contrived to make him a traditionalist rather than a revolutionary.

Lester was born in Woodville, Mississippi in 1909, and as if to mark the event his parents moved immediately to New Orleans, where Lester spent the first ten years of his life. He loved the atmosphere of the place, as he recalled in an interview late in his life:

See then, in New Orleans, they had them trucks that go round and advertise for a dance this night .. And this excited me, you know. So I'd be the hand bill boy. And I just loved that music, I'd be running till my tongue was just hanging out, like this.

There was music at home too, and plenty of it. Lester's father Willis, known as Billy, was a graduate of Tuskegee whose overriding ambition was to start a band with all the members of his family in its ranks. The Young children were taught to sing almost before they could form sentences. At the age of five they were started on their first instrument, in Lester's case the drums. Lester's mother played the piano and Billy Young was a multi-instrumentalist who focused on the trumpet.

He was also adept at wielding a rather less musical instrument – his leather razor strap, which would come into action when any of the children fell short of his strictly enforced musical standards. His insistence on sight reading and the authoritarian methods with which he backed it up planted an early seed of rebellion in Lester's mind. It also engendered his taste for spontaneity. The Billy Young Orchestra toured with small circuses in the Southern States, playing at pre-show parades and accompanying acrobats and bareback riders.

In 1919 Lester's parents divorced and Billy Young left New Orleans to work in Minneapolis taking the children with him. He married a baritone saxophone specialist and it is tempting to think that, for the obsessive Billy, his new wife's musical potential was just as important as her personal qualities. Around this time Lester switched from drums to alto-saxophone, principally because he found the drumkit cumbersome to carry about. His brother Lee dutifully replaced him and pleased his father greatly with this demonstration of commitment to the family band. Lee Young was a conventionalist who was constantly lionized in the family circle at Lester's expense. He went on to enjoy a rather middling career as a percussionist. Jazz historians following Lester Young's career used to seek out Billy Young towards the end of his life and invariably started their interviews by praising his marvellous son. Billy would reply gruffly that Lee was indeed a fine drummer, a solid citizen and was working on his golf handicap. To Mr Young Sr, Lee was the hero and success in the family. Lester, on the other hand, was merely mercurial, a troubling and puzzling nomad.

The friction between father and son meant that Lester finally did what he had often threatened to do, and left the family band behind forever. Minneapolis was not a great centre of jazz music, and he had to scratch around for work. He joined Art Bronson's Band which operated out of Salina, Kansas and it was with this outfit that he graduated to the tenor saxophone, the instrument upon which he was to make such a strong impact.

The most creative band in the region at this time was the Original Blue Devils whose base was south-west of Minneapolis in Oklahoma City. Lester joined up in 1932 and found himself in an outfit bristling with talent and inventiveness. Among the personnel was Count Basie, and many of those who were to join the great man's big band, like Walter Page, Eddie Durham and Jimmy Rushing. These men would later fulfil a crucial role in Lester's career. In 1932 though, the

Kansas City, a bland looking mid-western grain and cattle market town, became a major centre for jazz music in the 1930s.

The Depression ravaged America, but Kansas City suffered less than most places because of its importance as an agricultural centre. Its relative economic well-being made it a refuge for jazzmen.

Depression was biting hard, and the best musicians started to drift away from the Blue Devils in search of some sanctuary from the ravages of the slump.

At this time Lester demonstrated a trait that would recur with distressing regularity throughout his life – his almost total lack of acumen when it came to manœuvring himself politically to further his career. He chose to stay with the Blue Devils until the bitter end even though the band was slowly disintegrating around him. Basie and the others had already left when the Blue Devils went broke on a disastrous tour in the east and Lester was left to creep back penniless to Minneapolis, having shown a disabling mixture of misplaced loyalty and timidity.

There followed a stint with the great King Oliver, who was playing out his twilight years with an obscure ten-piece orchestra. Oliver, a fading star whose thunder had been well and truly stolen by his protégé Louis Armstrong, was beset by personnel and financial problems at this time, but Lester remembered him as unfailingly cheerful and courteous.

Lester was a light-skinned negro with deep green eyes, tall and rather elegant with the dreamy manner of a rebel. He certainly did not fit any stereotypes. By this time, he had found a voice on the tenor saxophone which was highly individual, contrasting strongly with the macho roar of Coleman Hawkins. He concentrated on the higher registers of the instrument, making it sound light and poetic. He also played without vibrato. Lester developed his style partly by listening to a white saxophonist called Frankie Trumbauer who played in Bix Beiderbecke's band. Beiderbecke, a white boy from Iowa, was a cornet player of prodigious talent. who first came to prominence in the Paul Whiteman Band and then moved on to Small Group work. He produced jazz of limpid poise and great melodic beauty, polishing each note until it sounded like the chime of a bell. His relaxed, spacious style could be considered as the first manifestation of a 'cool' approach to a music which until then had been fast and furious. Bix died at the age of twenty-eight in 1931, destroyed by alcohol addiction and tragically unfulfilled. Trumbauer was a C melody saxophone specialist, an instrument which is now obsolete but was a sort of half-way house between tenor and alto-sax. Lester was fascinated by Trumbauer's floating, ghostly tone and

emulated it on the tenor. By doing so he developed a musical voice
that suited his gentle and evasive personality, a style which was not to
everyone's taste, as he was soon to discover.

In 1934 he was playing once more with Bill Basie in Little Rock.
Fletcher Henderson was in the audience and was impressed enough to
offer Lester a job on the spot. Henderson's orchestra was highly
successful and Lester jumped at the opportunity. Unfortunately for
Lester he had been booked to replace Coleman Hawkins – the
embodiment of everything he had reacted against stylistically. When
Lester got up to play the band could hardly believe what they heard.
To their ears it was not a deft and poetic style, it was just weak and
pallid. They wanted no part of him no matter what Henderson
thought. To their discredit they started a very effective whispering
campaign against Lester. He could not stomach it and left after only a
few months, bruised and insecure.

Back in Minneapolis again, Lester was twiddling his radio dial in
search of music when he picked up a broadcast from the Reno Club
featuring a group led by his old friend Bill Basie. Acting with
uncharacteristic alacrity, Lester fired off a telegram asking for a job,
and the response was immediate and positive. So Lester left
Minneapolis and made Kansas City his base. He had married and
took his wife Beatrice with him, but the marriage was to fail very

quickly and rather mysteriously: Lester never spoke about Beatrice, nor of what went wrong, even to his closest friends.

Kansas City was one of the best-kept secrets of jazz history. It was run by a corrupt, easy-going democrat called Tom Pendergast who operated as if Prohibition had never been thought of. He managed to exploit the city's pre-eminent position as a wheat and cattle market to insulate it from the ravages of the Depression. It was as a by-product of this policy that Kansas City became a centre for entertainment and music. This was the sanctuary found by the fleeing Blue Devils musicians when they drifted away from the band. Kansas City was a honeycomb of nightclubs, cabarets, speakeasies and dance halls where music could be heard from early evening until dawn, when informal jam sessions took over. It was during one of these sessions that Coleman Hawkins and Lester Young finally locked horns musically. The black novelist Ralph Ellison, who was raised in the south-west, recalled that the contest was gladiatorial in its ferocity, and resulted in Lester outthinking and outplaying Hawkins who left the stage battered and defeated. A less insecure man than Lester would have taken this victory as a signal to put the Fletcher–Henderson incident behind him.

Jazz in Kansas City had a unique style that suited Lester very well. Perhaps it was the sense of space engendered by the plains of the mid-west that led to a more relaxed and informal music, less dependent on the tight ensembles typical of New Orleans or Chicago. What is more, the geographical isolation of Kansas City, far from the post-slave culture of the south and the proto-ghetto culture of New York or Chicago meant that it escaped the worst aspects of racism.

One of the most important venues in the city was the Reno Club. This was where Lester joined the Basie Band and finally found his feet. Every night when Lester stepped up to play, a precocious teenager watched and listened intently. He would repeat Lester's fingerwork in the thin air in front of him, imitate the master's breathing patterns, and on his way home he would try to commit to memory the solos he had heard. Lester Young was a hero to this stocky, unprepossessing young man and would remain so until his premature death. The name of the devotee was Charlie Parker.

Also drawn to the mid-western metropolis were some of the more astute talent scouts and record producers of the time. One of them

was a well-to-do, middle-class white man called John Hammond. Like
Lester, he had heard the Reno Club broadcasts on the station W9XBY,
which, because of its good strong signal, Hammond had picked up in
Chicago where he was looking after Benny Goodman. He came to
Kansas City expressly to sign up the Basie group. Typically of
Hammond, but it has to be said rather untypically of most producers
of the time, he informed Basie of his rights, offered him good
advances and a share of royalties. But he was too late. As a downcast
Basie explained to Hammond, a man from Decca, called Dave Catt,
had already signed him up to a deal without royalties. What is more,
Catt had deceived Basie into thinking the fee for the whole band was
in fact the individual fee for each musician.

So Basie had no choice, and the band went off to Chicago to
record. They managed to secure a residency at the Grand Terrace in
the City to help their finances a bit. Given Decca's treatment of Basie,
Hammond had absolutely no scruples about putting together a small
Basie group to do some bootleg recordings. It comprised Basie on
piano, Jo Jones on drums, Walter Page on bass and Lester Young on
tenor sax with Jimmy Rushing as the vocalist. Hammond concocted
the none-too-convincing name of Jones Smith Incorporated for the
band to record under.

On 8 October 1936 around breakfast time the group emerged from
the Grand Terrace and made its way furtively to a small Chicago
recording studio. The first-choice trumpet player Buck Clayton had
split his lip and was replaced at the last minute by Carl Smith. If that
seemed to bode badly for the proceedings, all gloom was lifted when
Lester played his first chorus on this, his very first recording. Up until
that moment his musical qualities had been known only to a few,
rather like the Kansas City scene itself. His style had been maturing in
the clubs of that city like fine wine in a cellar, and in 1936 he burst
upon the world with a mature style that appeared to owe nothing to
anyone or anything that had gone before.

In fact, like all great innovators, he had absorbed influences from
all sorts of sources and transformed them into something original,
coherent and beautiful. First there was his light sinuous tone which
must have seemed unique, but which as we have seen he derived from
Frankie Trumbauer's C melody sax style. Then there was Lester's
rhythmic deftness. He jumped across bars with a breathtaking

freedom that was fleet and poetic. The influence in this case was his own childhood drumming, which gave him the knack of laying down a rhythm and playing against it at the same time. He was able to transfer these ideas to the saxophone with a remarkable felicity. Jones Smith Incorporated had developed a fresh approach to their raw material. Although they relied on the usual repertoire of blues and tin pan alley (Gershwin's *Lady Be Good* was particularly striking in this first session) they did not always start with an ensemble statement of the main melody, instead they went straight into solo articulations of poetic complexity. It sounded exciting, and in a way abstract. This approach was derived from the Kansas City and south-western 'cutting' contests that had done so much to form Lester's style, but which were unfamiliar among east-coast jazz fans.

Charlie Parker, the teenage spectator at the Reno Club, would, when his own career took off, exploit the rhythmic freedoms Lester had so elegantly sketched out and add an audience-defying cocktail of harmonic exploration. Lester's oblique approach to his raw material was something that Parker appreciated, and built on.

The formation of the definitive Count Basie Big Band followed in 1936 soon after the Jones–Smith recordings. It played like a well-oiled machine and its punch and verve provided a bracing antidote to Lester's dreamy lyricism. Basie's musical discipline was something that Lester could understand, and looking back to the abject acquiescence demanded of him in his family band, it all seemed like a bad dream, as he recalled in an interview recorded towards the end of his life.

The glittering sound of the full Basie Band provided a marvellous background out of which Lester's solos could surge in thrilling moments of pure drama. Count Basie even managed to make the most of Lester's unusual personality and musical style in the band's stage act. He sat Lester at one end of the tenor section and a Texan saxophonist called Hershel Evans who was all honking bluster – Coleman Hawkins plus, you might say – at the other end of the section. The two men swapped highly contrasting solos that sounded like furious musical arguments. So dramatic was the effect that it was even put about, quite erroneously, that Lester and Hershel were sworn personal enemies.

During this creative period of his life Lester married his second wife, Mary, and they were happy together until the war years

intervened. While working with Basie, he was pursuing a parallel
career with a small band put together by John Hammond to
accompany the great blues singer Billie Holiday. The beautiful
recordings they made are as seminal in their way as the
Armstrong–Bessie Smith collaboration of the previous decade. Billie
Holiday's poignant, vulnerable voice sounded, on occasions, for all the
world like Lester's horn speaking. The musical empathy between them
was extraordinary: they listened to each other, swapped phrases, and
embroidered each other's ideas. According to Buck Clayton, the
trumpeter on these sessions, although Billie and Lester were never
romantically inclined, they shared a platonic love and deep friendship
from the moment they set eyes on each other. It was a relationship
that helped sustain two vulnerable artists in a potentially hostile world
and which lasted until Lester's death. The private names they had
invented for each other were to become legendary: Lady Day was

Big bands liked to compete
with each other to see
who could 'swing' most
effectively. This poster
advertises a particularly fine
double bill in New York in
1938: Chick Webb and
Ella Fitzgerald, followed
by Count Basie and
Billie Holiday.
Opposite, Lester Young
holding his tenor at the rakish
angle usual for him, with
Count Basie on piano and Jo
Jones on drums at the
Apollo in New York in 1940.
Below, living her song: Billie
Holiday in her prime

Lester's name for Billie, while she dubbed him 'Pres' – the President of
the tenor sax, a soubriquet that few would have denied him at this
point in his career. They also enjoyed smoking pot together – in fact,
they threw up any smokescreen that would hide their bohemian
habits from the conventional world.

In 1940 Lester left the Basie band, although the reason for the split
remains shrouded in mystery: according to the leader's public
pronouncements, they parted on the best of terms and indeed this
claim is born out by the fact that Lester rejoined Basie at the
beginning of 1944. In the meantime he went to California and stayed
with his brother Lee while he endured a frustrating wait to get a union
card. Lester's mood was not helped by Lee's ultra-suburban home with
its back yard where his brother practised his golf shots. When Lester
did eventually get to record in 1942, with a group which included Nat
King Cole on piano, he unveiled a much heavier tone on the tenor
sax, full of vibrato and much more conventional. In short, he sounded
less his own man. Just after this recording Billie Young died, perplexed
to the end by his son Lester, just as Lester remained hurt by his
father's rejection.

Things began to improve when he rejoined Count Basie. Lester's
growing stature in the musical world was confirmed by a rather
pretentious, sepulchrally-lit short film called *Jammin' the Blues*, which

A still from the short film
Jammin' the Blues starring
Lester Young and made
in 1944

opened with the top of Lester's iconic pork pie hat in full frame as the saxophonist gazed down at the floor. There is every reason to believe that Lester lived up to the sort of bohemian image of himself presented in this most arty of art films. He had developed a highly personal and oblique language that pervaded the jazz world. Many claims, some of them vague and inflated, have been made about the linguistic originality of black American English, but in the case of Lester Young's language, such claims seem to have some substance. Buck Clayton believed Lester coined the usage of the word 'bread' to mean money, when he asked of a job 'How does the bread smell?' To express his own hurt feelings he would say he had been 'bruised' – a frequently heard word in the Young vocabulary. Another favourite expression was 'Ivey Divey' which signalled a rather bleak, stoic acceptance of some misfortune. Lester also used the title 'Lady', which he had bestowed on Billie Holiday, as a rather unnerving handle to the names of male friends and colleagues. It was a habit which along with his rather languid, camp manner, gave the wholly inaccurate impression that he was homosexual.

There is a kind of perverse innocence about these productive pre-war years which makes the manner of their shattering all the more brutal. In 1944 Lester was playing with a Basie colleague, the drummer Jo Jones in California. Jones recalled that between sets they were approached by a friendly young man who seemed eager to discuss jazz. After chatting for a while he bought the musicians a drink. It was then that he pulled out an FBI badge and served them papers instructing them to report to the local army induction centre the following morning.

Private 39729502 Young's army career was to say the least not a distinguished one. Terrified of the rigid military discipline which seemed like a nightmare journey back to his regimented childhood, he habitually drank himself into oblivion and into deep trouble with the powers that be. Incredibly inept at physical training, he dislocated his shoulder on an obstacle course and needed minor surgery. Hashish was discovered on Private Young's person in the military hospital and he was courtmartialled. The sentence was dishonourable discharge after a year's confinement at Fort Levensworth, Texas. This unpromising sojourn was made tolerable by the happy chance that fellow musician Gil Evans, the man who was to team up with Miles

Davis after the war, was also based at Levensworth. When he heard of Lester's confinement he did all he could to help the tenor player.

To ask why Lester could not deal with these repeated blows to his self-esteem – his father's razor strap, malign whispering in the Fletcher Henderson band, disciplinary confinement in the US army – is to beg the psychological question. If he had not suffered from an inner weakness that made these events significant in his eyes, they would not have seemed such hammer blows of fate.

When he returned to the civilian world in 1945, Lester was not the man he had been. His second marriage failed and it is tempting to regard his post-war career as a harrowing slide towards a death that was a virtual suicide. But this would be an over-simplification. Days after his release he recorded one of his favourite pieces, *DB Blues*, (*Detention Barracks Blues*), a record in which he packs a formidable and authoritative swing. Another hit followed soon after: a blues riff called *Jumping with Symphony Sid* which was dedicated to the influential disc jockey and promoter of be-bop Sid Torrin, and was Lester's nod to the rampant new movement. Around this time he married for the third time, to a second Mary, and set up house in Queens.

Things were not looking too bad for him at this point. but somehow they just did not work out. For one thing, the jazz scene had changed radically. A dispute which had dragged on for several years between the Musician's Union and the major record companies had hidden the emergence of major new talents. When the enterprise of a few small independent recording companies made jazz available again, it became clear that Lester's role as the great innovator had been well and truly usurped by the alto-saxophonist Charlie Parker. The strident iconoclasm of be-bop had caught the public imagination and Lester began to think that his more stealthy revolution had been forgotten. In an all-star concert at the Los Angeles Philharmonic Auditorium organized by Norman Granz just after the war, Lester played alongside Parker. Not recognizing him as the youth who had been his teenage admirer, he was distinctly wary and defensive.

If he felt that revolution had toppled him he also suspected that emulation had diminished him. A new generation of tenor players who had modelled themselves on him during the great Young–Hawkins schism, had come to maturity. It was not that players like Dexter Gordon, Wardell Gray or Stan Getz were simply stealing Lester's ideas. They had learnt from him and acknowledged as much. Some might have regarded this as a measure of esteem but Lester reacted more like the poet William Blake:

I found them blind
I taught them to see
And now I know
Neither themselves nor me.

Lester could not impose himself as a leader, either on or off the stand. He just was not that kind of person. There were ominous signs of all this during the pre-war break he had from the Basie band in California. Although he could inspire with his musical genius, all those traits that seemed attractive in the younger man, his dreaminess, diffidence and evasiveness became a tiresome liability when it came to leading a band and being responsible for other people, in short, trying to make a living in the real world.

This kind of failure was not lost on Lester, who was only too ready to recognize his own shortcomings. As usual his response was defeatist. He became more and more withdrawn and began drinking heavily. As a result he played less well which made him more miserable and so the downward spiral continued. There was the occasional sign of recovery, like *Pres Returns* which he recorded with Teddy Wilson, the pianist who had played on the pre-war Billie Holiday sessions. On this record his old inventiveness seemed to return but this was atypical. Usually Lester struggled just to keep going. Sometimes his playing was so bad it was reduced to a series of feeble honkings desperately strung out until the end of a solo. His breathing, a vital part of any reed-player's technique was beginning to go. The beautiful, sinuous solos of Lester's prime were no more. It was rather like a wonderfully honed athlete going to seed.

A session recorded for television in 1957 bore poignant witness to the depths of Lester's problems. He teamed up for one last time with Billie Holiday, who, by this time, was also in poor shape. Her despairing features, like those of Lester were coarsened by heavy drinking. But despite everything their extraordinary musical empathy had not diminished, and it was rekindled in a ghostly echo of the beautiful recordings of fifteen years earlier. The number was called *Fine and Mellow*, a title the irony of which would certainly not have been lost on either of them. Billie's voice faltered desperately through the chorus, and when Lester stood up to play he was so weak he nearly stumbled. There followed a chorus which almost expired as it proceeded, so weak was the execution. And yet there was a strange beauty about it: a perfectly conceived and regretful farewell. Time was indeed running out for the President as it was for his Lady Day.

Lester had been maintaining the semblance of a home life with Mary and their son, Lester junior, back in Queens, but with his constant drinking this too came under threat. The real danger sign for Mary was when her husband began losing interest in food. As usual Lester retreated from the situation. Feeling he had nothing left to offer his wife and son, he moved out of the family home and checked into a shabby, mock-gothic hotel on 52nd Street and Broadway, called The Alvin. From his room he could look directly down on Birdland, the club named after Charlie Parker. Friends were alarmed at Lester's masochistic choice of abode but his unconvincing response when they voiced their concerns was that he needed to focus on Birdland to gain inspiration. In fact all he did was to turn Parker, whose brilliant career had already burnt itself out in early death, into another of those demons who had haunted and taunted him all his life. Lester could have used Birdland as an inspiration, he could have regarded it as a reminder of the continuity of jazz and of his own triumphs in the Reno Club in Kansas. But he chose to see it as the final nail in the coffin. So, he sat on his balcony looking down at Birdland, drinking his fearful cocktails of gin and sherry, brooding and feeling he had outlived his time.

Lester still had friends who cared and worried about him. They introduced him to a sympathetic physician whose speciality was alcoholism. Dr Luther Cloud was definitely Lester's last chance. He was able to get very close to the saxophonist in the last few months of his life partly because the doctor was a jazz fan who knew his patient's worth, but also because of the medical and psychological skills he possessed. Cloud worked hard trying to control Lester's drinking, and Lester, he said, took it beautifully. But the physical and mental damage the jazz man had suffered were too severe and all Dr Cloud could do was to slow down the decline.

Opposite, Lester Young photographed in Paris in 1959 during his last disastrous residency. The Pork Pie Hat he liked to wear featured in the title of Mingus's tribute composed for Young when he died about a month later.

During a car ride with his old friend and fellow saxophonist Buddy Tate in 1958, Lester said that he thought his life as a musician had been a failure. 'The other ladies made all the bread,' as he put it. Lester's grasp on life had become slight indeed.

Fate was to throw Lester Young one last illusory chance. He was offered a month's residency at the Blue Note in Paris and with it the hope of rebuilding something of his reputation. But the hope was still-born. Away from Dr Cloud and supportive friends, stuck in a city he did not understand and playing with a rhythm section he hated, Lester took comfort in absinthe, the highly potent and toxic drink once favoured by Baudelaire. It was really the last thing he needed as he admitted during one of his regular phone calls to Dr Cloud. Unsurprisingly, the residency was a failure and was terminated by mutual consent after just three weeks. Paris had been as disastrous for Lester as it had been triumphant for Bechet.

Lester was now suffering from varicose veins in his stomach, and during the long flight home he bled internally, arriving in New York in desperate shape. He needed a hospital, friends, or even his home at Queens. Instead he headed back to his solitary room in The Alvin. The people at the hotel tried desperately to contact Dr Cloud, but luck had run out for Lester. It was a Saturday, and the doctor was playing handball in New Jersey. Driving back to New York, Dr Cloud, who did not even know Lester was back in the country, heard on his car radio that the renowned jazz man Lester Young had just died in a New York hotel.

Just a few blocks from The Alvin, Charles Mingus, the influential band leader, was playing with a small group, when someone came to the bandstand and whispered the news to him. Mingus paused and then started to improvise the slow blues that came to be known as *Goodbye Pork Pie Hat*. Lester Young's reputation as a jazz innovator has been obscured by the melancholy profile of his career. The fact that he produced his most original work when he was about thirty years old, and that the last twenty years of his life were little more than a footnote to a brilliant pre-war flowering, has led critics to mark down the influence he had on the development of jazz music. In fact he single-handedly transformed the saxophone style created by Coleman Hawkins and inspired Charlie Parker.

7

Charles Parker warming up
for the Paris Jazz Festival in
1949. It was this festival that
saw him 'jamming' with
Sidney Bechet.

*He stopped by my place a number of times. He
was like a child with the shrewdness of a child.
He possessed tremendous enthusiasm. He'd come
in and explain, 'Take me as you would a baby
and teach me music. I only write in one voice.
I want to have structure. I want to write
orchestral scores.'*

Edgar Varèse, composer, speaking in 1955

Charlie Parker

Charlie Parker is often portrayed as the genius who came out of nowhere, an individualist of such innate gifts that he was unformed by any tradition or precedent. In fact, as we have seen, the teenage Parker was an avid student of the Lester Young style. One of the earliest solos Parker ever recorded was of the Lester Young vehicle *Lady Be Good*. If the record is slowed down, the sound of Parker's alto transforms itself into an exact note-for-note copy of Lester's solo of 1938. Parker had absorbed Young's rhythmic daring and poetic approach to melody, and built on them to produce be-bop.

Charlie was also formed in a more general sense by the jazz culture of Kansas City in the Pendergast era. He was born in a suburb of the city in 1920, his father was a feckless singer and dancer whose vaudeville career was already on the skids, his mother was a doggedly loyal, self-abasing woman, who put more and more of her emotional capital into Charlie's upbringing as her husband's professional life unravelled into desperate obscurity, and his presence at home became increasingly intermittent. Consequently, Charlie was never told off, never even reined back, and there remained in his behaviour something of the spoilt brat until his premature death in 1955.

When Parker was about eight years old, the family moved from the suburbs to a house on Olive Street in the black quarter of town. The new home was almost within earshot of the jazz clubs which were so active and enterprising in the Pendergast era. Before long Charlie's father had dropped out of the family scene altogether, and his much put upon wife, Addie, worked all the hours she could as a domestic help so that her son could get a good education. At Lincoln High School Charlie was alert and unusually bright, and he was quick to realize that the school was not up to much. This quickly undermined his interest so that his attendance became patchy, his grades poor.

Fortuitously for Parker, the only strong discipline Lincoln High could offer was music. The school had a tradition of marching bands, and Charlie signed up. Like most beginners he was given a baritone saxophone to nurse as he brought up the rear of the column but before long Charlie had asked his mother if she could buy him the instrument that really took his fancy: the alto-sax. It was much more versatile and expressive than the baritone and Parker was fascinated by its light, intimate tone. Mrs Parker raided her modest savings and managed to scrape together enough money to buy a beaten-up, leaky old instrument made in Paris in 1898. It was good enough, though, to open up an extra-curricular musical career for Charlie, with a band called the Deans of Swing which was made up of Lincoln pupils and which played dance dates in the Kansas area. Charlie was fourteen, and as band activities absorbed more and more of his time, his school attendance became virtually non-existent.

Charlie's truancy and frantic precociousness continued when Mrs Parker took a cleaning job in downtown Kansas that involved working nights, which left him unsupervised from midnight until eight in the morning. Incapable of thinking any ill of her son, Addie Parker was quite untroubled by the prospect. Charlie was quick to exploit the situation. Dressing up in a long coat, with a fedora pulled over his eyes and a cigarette held at a rakish angle, he talked his way into the local jazz clubs with a mastery of jazz slang that disguised his age. There he could listen to Ben Webster, Herschel Evans and above all, Lester Young jamming into the night. Before long the Deans of Swing began to lose their allure.

The precociousness that marked Parker out deprived him of a proper childhood and adolescence. Like many who have lost out in this way, he was haunted in later life by the sense of never having properly grown up. He was impatient to infiltrate the jazz scene, but not even he thought that he was ready for the Sunset or the Reno or any of the other clubs where the big guns played. In any case, they would not have let him improvise with them. He soon got a chance to jam at an obscure club called the High Hat. It was revelation, not of genius in the making, but of how little musical theory Charlie had acquired. He came a cropper during a solo in *Body and Soul* because, amazingly, until that moment he had not realized that all tunes were not in the key of C. He went home humiliated and spent the next month or so painstakingly learning and practising the twelve major keys. Had he asked anyone, he would have discovered that most jazz

players limited themselves to three or four keys, but he acquainted
himself with every single one. This mixture of ignorance and
arrogance provided the basis for the extraordinary harmonic fluency
that would characterize his best work.

Having furnished himself with a union card, Charlie got his first
paid job in a band led by the pianist Bill Channing. At the age of
fifteen he was a professional musician and a husband: he had married
Rebecca, a local nineteen year-old who was expecting his baby. Rebecca
moved into the Parker home at Olive Street, where she and Addie
started a competition to try and domesticate Charles Christopher
Parker. They both failed. The sexually incontinent and chaotic nature
of his personal life was already beginning to make itself felt.

Parker's real interests lay elsewhere and on the jazz scene things
were changing. Count Basie and a few other big Kansas City names
had been lured away to Chicago or the east coast, leaving room for
some different alignments back in Kansas.

Armed with a new alto-sax Charlie Parker joined an orchestra
formed by Tommy Douglas, a saxophonist with a very sound
theoretical and technical pedigree, but with limited expressive powers.
Douglas could see that Charlie was almost totally unschooled, but he
admired the young man's seriousness about music and took him under
his wing. He taught Parker to practise on a clarinet so as to improve
his fingering, and explained how different reeds could be used to
obtain different tones. Charlie knew virtually nothing about these two
vital aspects of saxophone playing. Douglas was a sort of father-figure
who gave him his first real musical apprenticeship.

Buoyed up by Douglas's interest, Charlie decided it was time to
jam again. This time the location was the prestigious Reno Club.
Basie drummer Jo Jones was on the stand, and anyone who was
anyone in the Kansas City jazz scene was in the audience. Charlie's
turn came with *I Got Rhythm*, and he swiftly delighted his
discriminating audience by pulling off a difficult key change.
Adrenalin pumping he tried an even more daring transition, faltered
and fell silent. Jo Jones's judgement was instant: he threw a cymbal
across the stage which crashed at Charlie's feet. The young man's ideas
were still running far ahead of his ability to execute them.

Parker spent the summer of 1937 doing a job at Lake Taneycomo in
the Ozarks. It was undemanding work, and while other musicians

took advantage of the boating and swimming, Charlie continued his
obsessive and solitary harmonic exercises, committing Lester Young
solos to memory for light relief and in the process wearing out the
grooves on the Jones Smith records he had taken with him.

He returned to Kansas City where Mayor Pendergast was the
subject of fraud and tax evasion investigations. It would only be a
matter of time before his political machine was dismantled. The jazz
world that had flourished under the politician's benign despotism was
under threat. Charlie was suffering as well. Constant squabbling
between his mother and wife was wearing him down, so he decided
to pawn his saxophone and take off for New York.

If it was dismal at home it was no better in the Big Apple. When
he arrived, Parker scrounged a bed off an acquaintance from Kansas
City, until he made himself so unpopular he got kicked out. So he
was forced, for the only time in his life, to take a non-musical job. He
worked as a dish-washer in Jimmy's Chicken Shack in Harlem –
unpleasant work that nevertheless was to have two big advantages,
one gastronomic, and one musical. In the first place Charlie could
have all the chicken he could eat. He had a huge appetite, but unless
food was placed under his nose he often went hungry through sheer
indolence. At the Chicken Shack it was available all day. Charlie ate a
lot of chicken and consequently from around this time the nickname
'Bird' or 'Yardbird' began to stick. Second, the great pianist, Art
Tatum was playing on the premises. Tatum, a prodigiously talented
musician had taught himself everything there was to know about the
piano. He had the touch of a concert pianist and the inventiveness of
a composer, and yet everything he did was rooted in jazz. Charlie
listened, fascinated, as the blind pianist worked quotations from one
tune into another. For example, *Goodbye Forever* would suddenly pop
up in the middle of *The Man I Love*. Parker stored away the musical
experience in his mind – a steel trap for such things – and his own
mature solos would be characterized by the mastery of musical
quotation and allusion learned from Tatum and which he went on to
refine into an improvisational technique.

Although he liked the feel of New York and sensed it was the place
to be, Charlie could only pick up the most demeaning of musical jobs
on this trip. Anyway, family called. He received a telegram from his
mother telling him to return to Kansas City for the funeral of his

father. Charles Parker senior had been knifed in a street fight and had
bled to death. The funeral was a dismal occasion, but in a musical
sense, Charlie's return was well timed. At the very moment when the
Reno and the Sunset clubs were being boarded up, the last of the great
Kansas City bands was being put together. The moving force was Jay
McShann, a boogie-woogie pianist. He and Charlie Parker had met
previously, and discovering that Bird was in town, McShann offered
him a job as lead alto-saxophonist. The pianist put together a talented
and individualistic group of musicians who produced an aggressive
sound; less smooth than Basie but more adventurous. Although be-
bop was essentially a small group phenomenon, the ground for the
movement was prepared by a fascinating series of short-lived
transitional big bands of which McShann's was the first.

McShann, moving away from Basie's predictable arrangements and
crisp swing, was stumbling towards be-bop harmony and rhythm,
albeit in the dark. It was the Dizzy Gillespie Orchestra that was to
emerge after the transitional period as the only fully fledged big band
embodiment of the be-bop idiom.

Parker's role in the McShann band was similar to that of Lester
Young in the Basie outfit, but Charlie was less of a team player than
Lester, and was more up-front about experimenting on the bandstand.
At the same time, Parker did not have the benefit of the small group
work that Lester had enjoyed, and for which the Basie man saved his
most innovative work. So Parker's influence on the McShann outfit
was much more noticeable and unsettling than Young's had been on
Basie's big band.

During a tour of the south-west in 1940, McShann was invited by
Radio KFBI to make a series of transcriptions. Charlie Parker's first
recorded notes date from this session and show just how well
developed a musician he had become. On *Honeysuckle Rose* he
combines Lester Young's flow with Art Tatum's attack, and throws in
some of the odd tricks with scales that fascinated him. His breathing
was already outstandingly well controlled and he stood out as the
most promising instrumentalist in McShann's talented band. He was
twenty years old.

Parker was also showing signs of astonishing receptiveness to the
sounds around him: the swish of car wheels, wind in the trees, a police
siren, they were all echoed and reworked in his solos. This kind of

openness was a musical version of what the poet John Keats called
'negative capability', and seemed in Bird's case to be inextricably
bound up with his inability to deal with daily life. To separate the
creative receptivity from the destructive waywardness was an
impossibility.

Before long the McShann band had been signed up by Decca,
mainly to churn out Blues numbers for their 'race' catalogue. One of
the sides they cut called *Hootie Blues*, ostensibly just a vehicle for
singer Walter Brown, featured an unidentified alto solo by Charlie
Parker of such originality and brilliance that the record became a cult
hit among jazz fans, who were forever swapping guesses about who
the gifted soloist might be.

When McShann played at the Savoy ballroom in Harlem, Charlie
attracted his first press notices, which were admiring of his technical
skill and lyric gifts. All in all, being back in Harlem had been a
gratifying experience for Parker, and when the McShann band left for
Kansas City, he was not on the bus. Having quit, he stayed on in the
city within a city that was to be his base for the remainder of his career.

While Parker had been feeling his way towards the be-bop idiom
within the context of McShann's band, more thoroughly articulated

The Jay McShann
Orchestra, which Charlie
Parker joined in 1940.
McShann is seated
at the piano, and Parker
is standing immediately
behind him, third from
the left.

experiments had been simmering away in some small group jam sessions in Harlem. It all started at a club called Minton's. This was just another rather drab music venue until its owner, Harlem businessman Henry Minton, decided to spruce it up and hired a manager to revitalize the music policy. The man he chose was Teddy Hill, a sound musician who had never excelled on the bandstand but who compensated by turning Minton's into the most prestigious after-hours jamming spot in the history of jazz. Hill became a sort of Diaghilev of jazz, a brilliant enabler of the brilliant. He started by hiring a highly innovative house rhythm section that comprised Kenny Clarke on drums, and Thelonius Monk on piano.

Clarke had developed an exciting and oblique rhythmic style marking the beat on the side cymbal and playing against it on the bass drum. Monk's piano style was arhythmic, odd and highly individual, rather like Monk himself. A reclusive man, he began his career on the gospel circuit and developed his own almost private musical language as an escape from the numbing ritual of religious declaration. By fragmenting the rhythmic and harmonic pulse underlying jazz, Clarke and Monk laid the foundations of the be-bop revolution. Their approach became a quicksand which swallowed uninnovative players, yet it brought nothing but the best out of those willing to listen and to experiment.

Minton's became an experimental jazz laboratory, attracting musicians as varied as Coleman Hawkins, Roy Eldridge, Art Tatum and Tadd Dameron. All they had in common was an interest in new ideas. One of the most talented of the younger players on the Minton's scene was the guitarist Charlie Christian who had worked with the Lionel Hampton Band and who was contributing vigorously to the new music until his immense promise was snuffed out by tuberculosis in 1942. When the classic be-bop quintet was put together a few years later, there was no guitarist. It almost seemed that if Christian was not available, no one else would do. Certainly his personal demeanour would have added a much-needed element of grace and calm to the be-bop movement.

It was at Minton's that the dadaistic name be-bop was first coined. It was borrowed from a phrase of scat singing in Louis Armstrong's 1927 number, *Hotter than That*.

Kenny Clarke had heard of Charlie Parker and went to see him play in another Harlem club which the altoist had made his base.

Impressed by his advanced rhythmic and harmonic ideas, Clarke invited Bird to join the jam sessions at Minton's. Dizzy Gillespie, a firebrand trumpeter who could play faster than any of the swing era players also began coming along at the same time. Before long the easy-going, transitional feel of Minton's was transformed into a fierce and combative modernism. Players of the older generation began to drop out as Gillespie and Parker tried ever more challenging tempos and keys. The almost mythic status of Minton's as a centre of innovation was enhanced because this period of far-reaching experimentation occurred during the recording ban that began in 1942. The dispute of the major record producers with the Musicians' Union meant that during this time jazz was virtually unheard by the American public. When a few independent producers finally secured a deal with the Union the jazz that emerged seemed miraculously transformed, like a butterfly emerging from a chrysalis.

Clarke had thought twice about inviting Parker to Minton's because the saxophonist appeared to be in such bad shape, living in chaos and squalor. The drummer found him somewhere to sleep and saw to it that he got regular food. Parker had been missing meals, partly because he had started taking heroin and the search for a fix became an imperative, while eating could always wait. This habit would stay with him until the last melancholy months of his life, when he seemed to give up everything. However, he had a strong constitution and could function quite well on the drug from day to day.

Parker married again at this time but Geraldine Scott made little impact on her husband's lifestyle and she was soon to leave him, as Rebecca had done before her. Clarke and some other musicians decided that, musical tastes notwithstanding, Parker needed the regular cheques, food and lodgings of a big band job if he was to survive.

The altoist was mentioned to Earl Hines, the great pianist who had played on Armstrong's Hot Five recordings and who at this time was leading a big band. Although Hines needed a tenor saxophonist Parker's innate musicality meant that a change to this instrument was no problem and Hines hired him without hesitation. Apart from Parker there were several notable modernists in the band, including Dizzy Gillespie. They enjoyed undercutting the arrangements with their odd, flattened notes and fierce, double-tempo solos. At the same

Following page, the unrecorded Earl Hines Orchestra, photographed at the Apollo Theatre, in 1943. Hines is at the piano and the vocalist is Sarah Vaughan. Dizzy Gillespie is the first figure on the left of the front row, and Parker, the first on the right.

time there were some truly old-fashioned musicians, like altoist John
Williams, whose quaint breathy attack would not have been out of
place in the King Oliver Orchestra. Thus it was that Hines's band
became an astonishing battleground of styles. Hines, a massive cigar-
smoking extrovert, seemed to enjoy the musical jousting: he was
certainly not just a traditionalist dupe of the modernist fourth column
within his ranks.

Parker's perfect musical memory even on an instrument he played
infrequently stood him in good stead when it came to dealing with
the complex arrangements of the band. He could learn a part from
one playing and throw his music away while others were still glued to
the notes. The leader often tried to catch him out but never
succeeded. However good the music, though, it was only a matter of
time before the Hines band pulled itself apart in a stylistic civil war,
leaving no legacy of recordings, much to the regret of jazz historians.

One of Hines's vocalists, Billy Eckstein, had the bright idea of
plundering the modernist players from the ruins of the great man's
band, adding some others, mostly graduates of the Jay McShann outfit
and creating an avant-garde big band. McShann hired Dizzy Gillespie
to lead the last of the transitional outfits and it also featured Charlie
Parker back on alto. Eckstein did not have much in the way of
prepared parts and often arrangements had to be sent by messenger
hours before a concert. The band lived from hand to mouth, but the
spikey modern idiom it created was highly original, echoing the
rhythmic and harmonic ideas that had come out of the small group
scene at Minton's. One of Eckstein's featured singers was the young
Sarah Vaughan, with whom Parker struck up a powerful musical
understanding.

However, Charlie sensed that he needed the intimacy of the small
combo to make his mark. Despite Eckstein's ingenious arrangements
they were a prison for the ambitious altoist, and he quit the band at
the end of a stint in New York. Parker had also sniffed out that there
was the chance of making a small group recording for Savoy, one of
the first independents to break the stalemate between the Union and
the major labels. These small companies were limited technically and
financially so they preferred working with small groups: for once
business considerations favoured the avant garde. The first Savoy
session nevertheless had a transitional feel about it. Art Tatum's

Jocular antics from Charlie
Parker and Dizzy Gillespie.
By the time this photograph
was taken in 1950, the two
were in reality distinctly
wary of each other.

guitarist Tiny Grimes put together a quartet with Parker on alto, to
back his vocal debut, which also turned out to be his vocal swansong
– it was lame and entirely forgettable. But the B–side instrumentals
Tiny's Tempos and *Red Cross* were Parker vehicles. The tricks hinted at
in the McShann transcriptions had matured into a beautiful
instrumental voice of great originality. Parker's reed tone, which was
at once lucid and intimate, gave a new edge to the alto sound. It was
without vibrato and was achieved by using a Rico Five – a very stiff
reed normally used only for military band work. It was exceptionally
hard to manipulate, and yet Parker could produce fluid runs of short
notes on it. An indication of the degree of his technical mastery as he
approached his first great period of creativity, is that many competent
altoists could only get a squawk out of a Rico Five. Parker was without
rival on the alto, the last innovator on the instrument being the great
Johnny Hodges, whose stately style remained rooted in the 1930s.

Meanwhile be-bop had established a mid-town home on Fifty-
second Street, where it was top of the bill for the first time, instead of
being an after hours experiment. It was here that Parker's definitive
be-bop quintet of trumpet, saxophone, drums, bass and piano
emerged. Parker's first trumpeter was Dizzy Gillespie, whose amiable
easy-going manner went down well with the fans and the music press.
The mercurial Parker soon resented this success and began to feel that
Gillespie was getting too much credit for the new music. However,
relations remained cordial, and the two men began to formalize their
compositional technique. It had started with the rhythmic tricks and
unpredictable harmonic modulations used at Minton's to scare off
old-timers. It developed into a fully fledged reworking of standards
which did away with the despised melodies, but retained the
emotional hook of the harmonic structure. So, *I Got Rhythm* became
Anthropology, and *Whispering* became *Groovin' High* and so on.
Extravagant claims have been made for the revolutionary nature of
this way of composing, but many of the be-bop numbers now sound
mannered and unconvincing. And in hanging on to the basic
harmonic structure while throwing out the recognizable tunes Parker
could be accused of perpetrating a pseudo-modernism, that sounded
fierce but relied to some extent on a saccharine tin-pan-alley
emotional 'hook'. In a way these compositions are the musical
equivalent of an insensitive refurbishment of an old house. One

exception is Tadd Dameron's *Hot House*, a be-bop classic, but
Dameron was a transitional musician with a 'reading' background
rather than an out-and-out be-bopper. Parker's stature as a jazz
composer is confirmed by his magisterial solo improvisations, and not
by the mannered, melodic statements that he devised as starting
points for his numbers.

With the major labels still silent, Savoy were in a position to lay
down the first definitive be-bop recordings in 1945. Parker was to be
joined by pianist Bud Powell, a young drummer in the Kenny Clarke
mould called Max Roach who was at the Manhattan School of Music,
and the young Miles Davis. Davis, who was studying at Julliard, had
already sat in with the Eckstein band when they played at his home
town of St Louis, and Parker had liked the burry tone of his trumpet
playing. Also, Davis hero-worshipped Parker, and did not steal the
limelight as Bird perceived Gillespie to be doing. As so often in the
be-bop bands, the bassist was a journeyman of limited ambition. On
this occasion it was Curly Russell. The session did not go smoothly.
Bud Powell did not show up, and was replaced by Dizzie Gillespie,
not one of the world's great pianists. Meanwhile, Bird had contacted
another stand-in pianist called Argonne Thornton who watched from
the control room. It soon became clear that Davis was rather overawed
by the occasion and was only too happy to stand down for Dizzy on
the fast numbers. This gave Thornton his chance to display his skills
on the piano. Dizzy played both trumpet and piano uncredited
because he had just signed an exclusive contract with another
independent, Musicraft.

The music was of the highest quality, with Parker's solos on *Now's
the Time* and a meditative blues called *Meandering* reaching the point
of perfection. On *Ko Ko*, Parker played at such a fast pace that there
was almost no time to accent and play with the beat. But he swang
like fury. To do so, Parker played notes which were so short that they
could hardly be conventionally notated. He played a cascading fall of
short notes in such a way as to trick the listener into 'hearing' a
resolving note that he did not actually play. It was a matter of timing
and weighing each note, and exploiting the ear's tendency to hear
what is expected even if it is not played.

The Savoy sessions established the basic be-bop formula of opening
statement played by trumpet and sax together, sax solo, trumpet solo,

Parker with some of the players he liked to play with most in the mid-1940s: Tommy Potter on bass, Miles Davis on trumpet and Max Roach at the drums

drum or piano flourish, and then a repeat of the opening statement to close the number. The trumpet and saxophone often developed a haunting inside-out harmony, that became the most immediately recognizable attribute of be-bop.

Sometimes many takes were necessary, as Miles Davis in particular struggled with the new material. Parker produced a different solo each time, never content to rest on his laurels, and sometimes taking great risks when anyone else would have settled for safety. That is why when Savoy re-issued the material from the Parker sessions in LP form, they included all the rejected takes, so that Bird's contribution could be fully appreciated.

One of the numbers recorded at this session was called *Billie's Bounce* a misspelt tribute to Billy Shaw, an enlightened and effective agent who had helped set up the Eckstein band. Shaw had taken the new music to his heart and did all he could to help Parker. He was a tough negotiator and yet was very forgiving of Parker's many misdemeanours. Except for the tribute, he got little thanks for either his commercial acumen or his compassion.

In 1945 Shaw saw an opportunity to spread the be-bop gospel to the west coast where a club owner called Billy Berg had expressed an interest in a Parker residency at his Hollywood bistro. The long trip was made by train, and half-way across the continent Parker began to suffer from heroin withdrawal symptoms. When the train stopped early one morning at a red signal somewhere in New Mexico, the hissing brakes and screeching wheels woke Bird out of a troubled sleep. He grabbed his coat and instrument case, opened the carriage door and set off at a brisk pace across the desert. He had walked about 500 yards beneath the cloudless blue sky before he got his first inkling of where he was, and headed back for the train. Heroin had started to exact its vicious price for the highs it had engendered.

In Los Angeles he found supplies of hard drugs unreliable. He played well at Billy Berg's when he had scored but suffered terribly when he had not. His residency scaled the heights and plumbed the depths. The same goes for the recordings Parker made with a west coast independent called Dial. Needless to say Bird had done nothing to inform Ross Russell, the owner of Dial, of his contractual arrangements with Savoy back on the east coast. The first session went well and included Parker classics like *Yardbird Suite* and *Moose the Mooche* named for Parker's hard-working Los Angeles drugs supplier.

Russell's second session produced a recording every bit as disastrous and poignant as Lester Young's *Fine and Mellow* some twelve years later. On *Lover Man* Jimmy Bunn's piano introduction seems endless as he covers for Parker's missed entry. When the saxophone finally comes in the tone is raw, anguished and the phrases unfinished though deeply affecting, as a dull-eyed and clumsy-fingered Bird struggled to articulate any sort of melodic line. But *Fine and Mellow* was Lester's painful farewell, whereas *Lover Man* was a nadir from which Bird would emerge to produce his finest work. For the moment though he had to be helped back to his room in the Civic Hotel where he was put to bed. Moments later he appeared in the lobby with no clothes on and tried to make a phone call. He got angry when staff and guests pointed out that he was naked, went back to his room and set fire to the bed.

In court, Parker was found guilty merely of 'disturbing the peace', but thanks to the intervention of Ross Russell and the trumpeter on the ill-fated *Lover Man* session, Howard Mcghee, Parker was sent to an enlightened and liberal institute at Camarillo, seventy miles north of Los Angeles. Bird spent the next six months recharging his batteries, eating well and even getting fresh air and exercise. Most important of all, he avoided the electrical therapy that might well have prevented him playing again. He came out in good shape and recorded one of his finest Dial sessions which included the beautiful *Cool Blues.* What Bird demonstrated in this masterpiece was the way that volume could be used as a way of expressing rhythmic ideas. Lester Young had contrasted honking bass notes with lithe runs during his solos in rumbustuous numbers and the effect was powerful but simply dramatic. Parker gave a subtly different weight to each note creating a sort of dappled effect. In fact, his use of volume to express rhythmic ideas was analogous to the way painters like Matisse used colour to express space.

If Parker was on untypically good form at this time, it was not just the good food and fresh air of Camarillo that he had to thank. While

Gouache on paper cut-out images from the sequence by Matisse entitled *Le Jazz* (1943). Parker's use of volume to express rhythm was a musical equivalent of the way Matisse used colour to express space.

he was still being treated there, a girlfriend from New York, Doris Syndor, came out to LA, took a job as a waitress and waited for Charlie's release. Then she devoted herself to looking after him. She was a shy, gawky girl whose relationship with Parker seemed based almost exclusively on trying to smooth his way. Like Charlie's mother whom she eerily resembled, she seemed happy to abase herself before his genius. Eventually they married, though there is no record of Charlie having taken the trouble to divorce wife number two.

When he flew back to New York, Parker found that be-bop had established itself. While he had been languishing in California, Dizzy Gillespie had been the subject of magazine profiles and network radio interviews. From this point the Parker–Gillespie relationship became increasingly wary on both sides. When they played together their rivalry produced musical duels of almost impossible technical bravura, as at the Massey Hall concert in Toronto. But Parker's more serious work was generally undertaken with Miles Davis and Max Roach, while the pianists and bassists came and went. Recordings with Savoy and Dial in 1947 produced some marvellous work, notably a version of *Embraceable You* a creation of lucid poignance recorded shortly after Parker had injected himself with heroin in the men's room of the studio. After the enforced abstinence of Camarillo, Bird was back on smack.

Not that he faced any major problems at this point. Be-bop was in the ascendant, Billy Shaw and Doris were on hand to look after his professional and personal life, he was winning polls and earning good money. But Parker's nihilistic instincts still prevailed. While playing a well paid gig at the elegant Argyll Lounge in Chicago, Parker finished a set, went into a phone booth in the foyer and urinated on the floor. It was one of innumerable similar incidents, the effect of which was to destroy what Shaw and Doris had been painstakingly building up.

Parker also had a compulsive habit of seducing women to degrade them. His was a psychotically destructive personality. But if there was one thing more objectionable than Bird's behaviour, it was the way jazz writers, mostly white ones, tried to justify it as 'black protest' or 'sexual honesty': it was neither.

One of the many oddities of Parker's life was his obsession with taxis. When he was in funds he would hire a cab for a whole day, cruise around Central Park with the seat piled high with unsigned, unread contracts. Parker often preferred sleeping in a yellow cab to sleeping in his own bed. He also used taxis to clinch many of his sexual encounters, giving a fresh meaning to the phrase 'the earth moved'.

In 1948 Parker made his last recording for an Independent record company. It was the Savoy session that produced *Parker's Mood*, a blues featuring alto, piano, bass and drums. Bird's magisterial opening statement had all the austere beauty of the most primitive examples of the genre. The intricate double-tempo clusters of notes that follow resemble the fast piano runs of Art Tatum, but instead of being just embellishments, they are perfectly integrated into the flow of the solo as a whole. There were five takes of *Parker's Mood*, each one more imaginative and daring than the last. Harmonic exploration and fragments of melody intersect like some three-dimensional mosaic. A few bars from home on the last take Parker starts to hammer home the final pieces of solo with the ease of genius.

The records Bird made after the Union conflict with the major labels was settled were certainly less distinguished than his work for Savoy or Dial. Often the line-up was foisted upon him by a producer with a commercial imperative. The independent record companies were the perfect vehicle for Parker's finest and most pure phase of music making. An interesting result of the more interventionist approach of the major labels was a session organized by Norman Granz for Mercury, featuring Charlie Parker with a chamber orchestra of strings and woodwind, comprising some players from the New York Philharmonic. To their credit, the orchestral musicians took the sessions seriously, and the sound of Bird's alto soaring above the orchestra was strangely compelling, despite its predictable denigration by many jazz purists.

Bird himself blew hot and cold about this work. Sometimes he thought it was just a bore, at other times he liked to think in a self-pitying and maudlin way that he had made jazz respectable. He dreamed of living in a fine house with a book-lined library, entertaining Stravinsky and Varese for dinner.

By the end of 1948, Parker's style of man management had so alienated Max Roach and Miles Davis that they quit. This left the way open for a second edition of the Parker Quintet, the personnel of which were quite a surprise. Bird's choice on trumpet was Red

Rodney, a Jewish boy from Philadelphia, who was joined by another
white musician on piano, Al Haig. Haig was a teetotaller with perfect
manners who looked like a school teacher.

Billy Shaw decided to launch the new quintet and raise Parker's
public profile by opening a club on Fifty-second Street to end all jazz
clubs. It was well appointed, and large oil paintings of great jazzmen
hung on the walls. Parker's own picture had pride of place.
'Symphony' Sid Torrin, a disc jockey from Radio WJZ who had done
much to make be-bop popular, was to broadcast live from the club
every night. Bird cages with tame finches hung from the ceiling and
the club was to be called *Birdland: The Jazz Corner of the World.* The
opening sessions with the new quintet went smoothly, much to
Shaw's relief.

Encouraged by this success the energetic agent managed to set up a
short tour of the southern states for Charlie, assuming that Rodney
and Haig would have to be replaced, as mixed-race bands were
unacceptable in the south. But Bird had the brilliant idea of passing

Bird at the Paris Jazz Festival
of 1949 with Max Roach.
Right, Parker with his fourth
wife, Chan, photographed in
1951. They were clearly well
suited to each other and
Chan even managed to
impose a conventional
domestic lifestyle on Parker –
for a few months.

them off as albino negroes. Haig would have none of it but Rodney was willing to give it a go. There followed a hilarious few weeks during which Rodney was ostentatiously presented as 'Albino Red' and Parker goaded white audiences by presenting himself as an 'educated nigger' and affecting high-flown syntax. He could mimic people as brilliantly as he could mimic sounds in his music. Bird ordered Rodney around imperiously, 'Hey boy, bring in those drums and see to my bags.' As far as the locals were concerned, Rodney was just the band rookey, but Bird was in fact wittily reversing racial stereotypes. Despite these jokes he was genuinely fond of Rodney. He even tried to warn him off heroin. Bird once told Max Roach that the purpose of his life was not primarily musical but to demonstrate the folly of taking hard drugs. Rodney, who wished to emulate Parker's music making, also emulated his lifestyle and took no heed of the advice.

On his return to New York in 1951, Charlie discovered that Doris had finally given up on him. He took up with an old girlfriend called Chan Richardson, who was from a well-heeled white family of bohemian inclination. When she became Mrs Parker number four she came closer than anyone to forming a satisfactory relationship with Charlie. For a while he lived a normal domestic life with Chan, and they had a daughter whom they called Pree. Charlie was thirty-four, and years of alcohol and drug abuse were beginning to slow him down. His weight had exploded and his face was coarsened and bloated. He was suffering from stomach ulcers.

A couple of whirlwind trips to Europe and a Mercury record date produced little of musical interest. Parker seemed to be playing on autopilot. On a trip to Philadelphia, Rodney was arrested for possessing narcotics, the quintet fell apart and Bird began to seem like yesterday's man. Then Charlie was devastated by the death of his daughter from pneumonia, and his mood darkened even more.

After a disastrous gig at Birdland, Parker went home drunk to be greeted by Chan's despairing assertion that she could not take any more. Bird went into the bathroom, drank a bottle of iodine and swallowed a load of aspirin. He was rushed to Bellevue Hospital where his stomach was pumped. Charlie was now frightening off prospective employers and family debts were mounting. In a mindless rage he stormed into Billy Shaw's office one morning, blamed him for

By the 1950s Parker was taking heroin, drinking heavily and eating compulsively. His weight shot up alarmingly as his health declined.

everything and switched to another agency. It quickly became clear what a tower of strength Shaw had been. At times the great saxophonist was reduced to hawking around his services as a freelance soloist, sometimes even paying people to let him play. Chan threw him out, and he squatted in an apartment devoid of basic facilities on Barrow Street, spending his days wandering aimlessly around Greenwich Village.

He got one last booking at Birdland. It was a chance to redeem himself with a band billed as The Charlie Parker All Stars. Parker arrived half an hour late to find his pianist, Bud Powell, also lately released from Bellevue, incapacitated by drink. Bird started abusing Powell for his mistakes over the PA. Powell swung around on the piano stool and shouted, 'What key, motherfucker?' 'The key of s for shit,' replied Parker.

Powell stormed off stage, leaving a morose Charlie Parker calling 'Bud Powell … Bud Powell …' into the microphone, as the club emptied. Thus ended the final gig at Birdland, the jazz venue designed to honour Parker's genius.

One of the few comforts Parker had in this last desperate year of his life was his friendship with the Baroness Pannonica de Koenigswater. This remarkable aristocratic free spirit from England had married a French count whom she had met while helping the Paris resistance during World War II. She then made New York her home, renting an elegant suite in the Stanhope Hotel on Fifth Avenue. An interest in jazz and a natural sympathy for the underdog led her to befriend some of the be-boppers, whose visits caused considerable consternation in the gilded and thick-carpeted lobby of the old-fashioned hotel. The jazz baroness was especially fond of the reclusive Thelonius Monk, but she also took Charlie Parker under her wing. For him the apartment was a sanctuary from the grinding discomfort of his daily life, and simply a place where he was valued.

On 9 March 1955, Charlie dropped in on the Baroness before travelling to a gig in Boston. Almost immediately he collapsed with acute stomach pains caused by enraged ulcers. The Baroness called in her physician Dr Freyman who made the diagnosis. After a lengthy examination he asked Bird if he drank much. 'Well doc, just the occasional sherry before dinner,' said Charlie. On the Saturday when he was meant to be playing in Boston, Charlie was propped in front

of the TV watching the The Tommy Dorsey Show. The mixture of
musical turns, tricks and gags was a pallid television version of the
vaudeville tradition to which Charlie's father had belonged. A
juggling act came on and Charlie laughed. Suddenly his throat was
full of blood and he choked to death as, on the screen, Dorsey picked
up his trombone to play *Marie*.

In his postmortem notes Dr Freyman estimated Parker's age at
about fifty-eight years. In fact he was thirty-four. During his last stay
at the Stanhope Hotel Charlie had quoted a stanza from the *Omar
Khayam* that seemed to haunt him:

Come fill the cup and in the fire of Spring,
Your Winter garment of Repentance fling;
The Bird of Time has but a little way
To flutter – and the Bird is on the Wing.

Comparisons between jazz musicians and classical composers are
generally meaningless, often thrown in to give some spurious prestige
to the improviser's art, and yet, in the case of Charlie Parker there are
some striking parallels with Wolfgang Amadeus Mozart, despite the
obvious cultural gulf separating them. The parallels are not directly
musical but reflect the way their lives and their music relate, or fail
to relate.

Both men were prodigiously and damagingly precocious and had
brilliant musical minds. They could express profound emotion in
their music while their personal behaviour could be infantile, even
callous. Their almost total indifference to the normal requirements of
everyday life is striking, as is their venality, the constant scramble for
money and the dizzyingly frequent moves of house. Bird had his own
Constanza in Chan. She once wrote in a letter, 'You can't expect any
gratitude from Bird 'cause anything he gets he feels as if it was
coming to him.' She understood his attitude without trying to
excuse it.

When Mozart died he was just one year older than Parker, but he
too was prematurely aged. Drinking had taken its toll and he was
worn out by money worries. Mozart, of course, was a functioning
social being, while Parker verged on the psychotic, but still the
similarities are striking.

Be-bop projected itself as being on the cutting edge of the jazz revolution. Its denigrators were quoted delightedly by its supporters to demonstrate just how great it really was. Philip Larkin's easy alliterative jibe at Parker, Pound and Picasso in *All What Jazz* has united modernists of all persuasions in opposition to it.

'How glibly I had talked of modern jazz without realizing the force of the adjective: this was modern jazz and Parker was a modern jazz player just as Picasso was a modern painter and Pound a modern poet.' Larkin went on to quote Benny Green's observation in *The Reluctant Art*: 'After Parker you had to be something of a musician to follow the best jazz of the day.' The grumpy poet fell on this comment with manic glee: 'Of course! After Picasso! After Pound! There could hardly have been a conciser summary of what I don't believe about art.'

For all the majesty of Parker's solos it is difficult to avoid the conclusion that the originality of be-bop has been somewhat over-rated. The tunes now sound dated and contrived, while the pattern of unison statement, two solos and unison closing chorus became stale and predictable. In a way Lester Young's small group works sound more timeless and less stereotyped.

Parker also robbed jazz temporarily of one of its chief glories, its collaborative creativity, whereby musicians could inspire each other to greater heights of improvisation. Parker did not really listen to his colleagues (he always tried to outplay Dizzy, but that is another matter). There is no record of his ever having made any sort of perceptive comments about any one else's playing. The Savoy LPs with their relentless cataloguing of retakes are in this respect almost like a ritual humiliation of Parker's sidemen. But the Parker solos that those retakes preserve were without equal and brought jazz to a new pitch of creativity.

8

Mingus photographed while
recording 'Let my Children...'
in New York in 1972

*He found his true place as a composer, which
was very similar to Duke's place as a composer.
Mingus poking fun at the players and giving
them problems to solve, it was a way of
bringing people right to the edge of their
capabilities, the far edge.*

Sy Johnson, pianist, in 1986

Charles Mingus

The bassist Charles Mingus was born only two years after Charlie
Parker. It might have been expected that his fierce musical ambition
would lead him to throw his considerable weight behind Parker's be
bop movement. The strength of Mingus's musical ambition though
was matched by a personal ferocity that verged on the reckless. He
was not inclined to be anyone's disciple, least of all a drug crazed
altoist from Kansas City. Mingus's tough independence of mind was
demonstrated when he moved to the east coast of America from his
native California in 1952. His career on the west coast had been
promising but fitful and the move had not changed his luck. Mingus
was already thirty when he joined the US Postal Service in New York.
He was gloomily reflecting on the prospect of delivering mail for a
living when he received a visit from Max Roach, the be-bop drummer
and close associate of Charlie Parker. Mingus had dropped Roach a
line in the hope of making some musical contacts in New York.
Roach responded principally because he was studying at the
Manhattan School of Music, located in the same district as Mingus's
apartment and it would make a convenient place to stop off after
lectures. The two men got on well and the visits became a habit; they
talked about music and what they wanted for themselves.

Mingus got his first big break through this friendship. A concert
was planned at the Massey Hall, Toronto, featuring Charlie Parker,
Dizzy Gillespie, Bud Powell and Max Roach himself. As Roach
explained to Mingus, Woody Herman's bassist Oscar Pettiford had
dropped out because he had injured an arm during a soft ball game in
Central Park between the Herman and the Basie bands. If Mingus
was interested, Roach would suggest him as a replacement. Mingus
was interested. There was no competition between being a postman
and playing with the finest musicians of the day at the Massey Hall.

However, the 1952 concert was not an encouraging introduction to
the be-bop scene for the newcomer. First of all, it had been scheduled
on the same night as the Rocky Marciano/Josey Joe Walcott

heavyweight championship fight and the hall was less than a third full. This was not the musicians' fault, but virtually everything else that happened that night was. Charlie Parker arrived without a saxophone and spent an hour cruising around town in a taxi until he found a suitable one to hire. Eccentrically, he settled on an alto made from white plastic. The pianist, Bud Powell, on the other hand had just been released from a sanatorium on Long Island, and was, not for the first time, alcoholically incapacitated.

When the concert started, Gillespie betrayed the growing edginess of his relationship with Parker by clowning about and leaving the stage every few minutes to catch up on the big fight. Goaded by this, Parker assumed a sumptuous 'Master of Ceremonies' accent and referred to Gillespie as 'My worthy constituent'. Mingus, a serious-minded man, must have wondered what he had walked into …

To mark his entry into the be-bop scene, Mingus had decided to record the concert backstage so that he could later release an LP. He had gone so far as to form a company with Max Roach for the purpose called Debut Records.

The concert produced some thrilling playing, despite the anarchic atmosphere, especially the musical duels that erupted between Gillespie and Parker, which had all the visceral excitement of aerial dog fights. Mingus noted all this on the playback, but he also found a couple of things which disturbed him. Firstly, he was dissatisfied with

Mingus playing at the famous Massey Hall concert in Toronto in 1953. Max Roach, who got him the gig, is on drums, and Dizzy Gillespie is on trumpet.

the distant pick-up on the bass, but worse, when the bass was audible, his playing was sometimes inaccurate. Before releasing the record he made sure he had redubbed his own part in its entirety. Mingus's first experience of be-bop was therefore unhappy both from a social and a musical point of view.

It was at another Charlie Parker concert that he was to bid a relieved farewell to be-bop. It was Parker's last gig at Birdland, a sorry affair which fell apart in a welter of drugs and alcohol (see previous chapter). Bud Powell was again alcoholically disabled and after a foul-mouthed row with Parker he stalked off the stage, leaving Bird stranded at the microphone pointlessly ordering Powell back to his piano as the club emptied. Showing uncharacteristic consideration for the audience, Mingus stepped forward and apologized for what he called 'the sick people' in the band. His farewell was a brave one because modern jazz *was* be-bop at the time, and his only other option was the US Postal Service. But still he sensed that for him, despite all its brilliance, be-bop was a cul-de-sac, not a way forward.

Mingus's ambition was to recreate the miraculously integrated rhythm section of the swing era. He aspired to the sort of intuitive ensemble playing displayed by Clyde Hart, Charlie Christian, Milt Hinton and Cozy Cole when they played in the Lionel Hampton Band in the late 1930s. In their hands guitar, bass and drums seemed to coalesce into one rich sound. For all its revolutionary fervour be-bop, in Mingus's estimation, had had an adverse effect on the rhythm section, and had set back bass playing a decade or so. The sort of arhythmical piano lines developed by Thelonius Monk and Bud Powell meant that the onus was on the bassist to hold the rhythm line like a good trooper. And in retrospect, much be-bop bass playing does sound unimaginative and staid. Mingus's rhythmic aspirations were simultaneously more rooted and more experimental than those of the be-boppers. But he was aware that if he re-established the unity of the rhythm section it would also have to carry the complex polyrhythms of modern jazz.

Charles Mingus was born in 1922, in a military camp at Mogales, Arizona where his army sergeant father was based. The family moved to Watts, the black suburb of Los Angeles. Although Charles's father was light enough to pass for white, Charles himself was a few shades darker and the extraordinary personal anger that fuelled him for most of his life seems to have been rooted in the sense of alienation that, as a coffee-coloured man, he felt. He did not belong in the white world and he did not feel that he belonged in the black world either. It was only through his music that he managed to bridge the gap between the black and white cultures.

Mingus's childhood was drab and uninspiring. Occasionally church music could be heard in the house, but that was all. One day when he was about six years old, Charles was playing with a radio set, and he picked up a broadcast of Duke Ellington's masterpiece *East St Louis Toodle-oo*. The effect was catalytic – the textures of the band and its rich, throaty orchestration enchanted Mingus and from that moment he focused on music. At school he showed a strong aptitude for musical theory which he studied voraciously. He also took up the cello, playing in the school orchestra and the Los Angeles Philharmonic Youth Orchestra. By this time Mingus had developed a strong interest in classical music which might have borne fruit but for the endemic racism in the world of music. Friends were quick to point out that he could not 'slap a cello' and that as a black man, or a man who would not ultimately pass for white, he had better take up the bass and play jazz if he wanted to work. It was good advice, although hardly likely to dampen down the fires of anger that were burning in Mingus's soul. He could not help but cast an envious eye from time to time at the Los Angeles Philharmonic.

Mingus embarked upon a first doomed marriage with Camilla Cross in 1944. They were divorced in 1947 when Charles began to mutter to friends about his own emotional inadequacy. However, his jazz career went well to begin with. Jobs with Louis Armstrong and Kid Ory were prestigious bookings for a beginner to land, even though the rather pedestrian bass line demanded by the New Orleans revival was not an inspiration to Mingus. His orchestral training as a cellist had influenced his ideas about the rôle of the bass in jazz, and he wanted it to play as powerful a part melodically as it had traditionally played rhythmically. As an instrumentalist, Mingus achieved this and he was very much his own man. Two other bassists had influenced him in his youth and convinced him that the bass could develop a new voice. They were the Californian, Red Callender, who had played with Charlie Parker, and the deceptively self-effacing Lionel Hampton, bassist, Milt Hinton.

There were not many precedents for bass players leading bands, but Mingus saw himself as a leader from the start. He was also keen to compose his own pieces. A California recording session in 1946 marked his achievement of both these ambitions. He led an eleven-piece band which included Lester Young's brother Lee on drums, and put down, among other things, two striking Mingus compositions: *Weird Nightmare* which announced Charles's lifelong taste for probingly pretentious titles, and an earthy blues called *Shuffle Bass Boogie.*

For a short time, in the late forties, Mingus actually billed himself as 'Charlie Baron Mingus'. The archaic line of New Orleans trumpet kings had expired, and 'Duke' Ellington and 'Count' Basie were both authoritatively established. This left 'Baron' as one of the few vacant and plausible titles in the mythical black music aristocracy, so Mingus grabbed it. However, his sense of the absurd was too strong for him to persist with this grandiose title for very long.

In any case, an offer to join Lionel Hampton assuaged the need for such self-justifying rhetoric. Mingus admired Hampton's band more than any other except Duke Ellington's, and the job gave Charles an introduction to the east coast scene which was much more musically vigorous than that in California. Hampton's band had swollen to gargantuan proportions by this time and the leader felt he needed two bass players to keep his musical pulse, so Mingus lined up alongside Joe Comfort. He swiftly convinced Hampton that he was under-employed as a mere second string bassist. Before long, the entire band was recording his composition *Mingus Fingers* which revealed Charlie's developing orchestration skills, as well as giving him a chance to display his instrumental talents.

Mingus played with his childhood hero Duke Ellington a few times in the late forties, but found it a surprisingly ungratifying experience. The two men were too close to each other musically and too wary of each other personally to hit it off. It did not help Mingus's confidence, and there followed a period of drift when he seems to have stopped playing.

It was around this time that Mingus married for a second time. Celia Zaentz was a very different person from Camilla Cross, and acted as her husband's manager. The same sort of tensions that had arisen between Armstrong and Lil Hardin plagued Mingus and Celia, but these were eased by a similar mutual respect and affection.

The Red Norvo Trio, which
Charlie Mingus joined in
1950: Tal Farlow on guitar,
Mingus on bass and the
leader on vibes

Eventually he was rescued from idleness by the white vibes player
Red Norvo who asked him to play in a trio which also included
guitarist Tal Farlow. So, leaving the epic scope and rich voicing of the
Hampton and Ellington bands behind him, Mingus joined one of the
most delicate, minimalist jazz chamber groups ever put together.

Mingus's work with this group is often overlooked, but it
constitutes a body of beautiful and precise chamber jazz. The trio
format pushed Charlie's bass into prominence, so that it could play a
melodic role as important as that of the vibes and the guitar, thus
fulfilling his early ambitions for the instrument. On these sessions
Mingus showed a surprising degree of respect for the sort of standard
tunes the trio played such as, *I've Got You Under My Skin,* and he
demonstrated what a sensitive listener he could be. It is largely due to
Mingus's innate melodic gift and strong jazz roots that the trio's
limpid chamber music managed to avoid the preciousness of the
modern jazz quartet, or the banalities of gutless cocktail jazz.

Mingus certainly did not look like a minimalist. By this time he
was a massively built man with huge upper arms, and a face which
could turn from thoughtful to glowering with alarming alacrity. He
was a big eater, ice cream being a particular obsession, and according
to his rather lurid semi-fictional autobiography *Beneath the Underdog,*
he had a fierce sexual appetite too. It seemed unlikely that Red
Norvo's genteel trio could contain such a personality for long, and
indeed, for whatever reason, Mingus went his own way after about
a year.

There followed the previously mentioned stint with the New York
Postal Service and the consequent colourful experience of the decline

and fall of Charlie Parker's be-bop empire. His experiment with be-bop may have seemed profitless to Mingus, but it had at least enabled him to establish his name on the east coast. What is more it probably helped him define more precisely what it was he wanted to do, by demonstrating to him that be-bop was not to be his musical idiom.

What Mingus needed was to find someone who shared his ambition to create an ensemble jazz for the post be-bop era. He found just that person in Danny Richmond, a young man from Greensborough, North Carolina. Richmond had just switched from tenor saxophone to drums, and perhaps it was his freshness, or even his inexperience, as a percussionist that helped him combine so effectively with the forbidding bassist. In any case, they hit it off together immediately, musically and personally. With Richmond, Mingus was at last able to start creating the sort of integrated modern rhythm section he had been dreaming about for so long.

So strong was their empathy when it came to rhythm that Richmond started to compensate for Mingus's tendency to stay right on top of the beat, by delaying his drum stroke fractionally. At a fast tempo this sounded like one fat resonant beat. On the bandstand their rhythmic mastery led to behaviour that must have seemed bewildering and chameleon-like to some of their colleagues. If the band was gelling too easily, Mingus would start obstructing things, muttering 'I don't want to swing like Count Basie, this is facile.' On the other hand, if the music was not catching fire, Mingus could transform the situation just by stomping his feet and shouting. This paradoxical attitude to swing was another illustration that the essence of jazz rhythm is conflictual. African polyrhythm fights the four beats to the bar derived from Europe, and for swing to live, a sort of balance must be maintained between the two.

Having solved his rhythmic problems, Mingus found that he was attracting the sort of individualistic instrumentalists that he needed, Ted Kerson on trumpet and Jimmy Knepper on trombone, players whose growling, vocalized tones suited Mingus's orchestration. It was another version of the instrumental approach first heard in New Orleans and then so effectively stylized by Duke Ellington in his 'jungle sound' of the 1920s.

Like Ellington, Mingus gave his instrumentalists a marvellous platform on which to display their talents, but also like the Duke, he was setting up a potential conflict between the band's needs and the individual musician's ambitions – and the bassist certainly did not have at his disposal the Duke's suave and laid-back style of man management.

By the end of the 1950s Mingus, now in his late 30s, was treating audiences to rather ostentatious displays of his fierce temper. He gave a series of presentations that went under the name of The Mingus Jazz Workshop and jazz fans began to feel that they had not got their money's worth unless the leader stopped the band in mid-flow a few times and bawled somebody out. There was an element of self-dramatization about all of this, which Mingus, as a canny operator and good businessman, was exploiting. After all, he was anticipating the fashion for improvization and audience participation which was soon to sweep through the theatres off Broadway.

Mingus's anger was real enough, however, and could erupt into violence. Once, when he was working on a large-scale piece with the trombonist Jimmy Knepper, he found himself augmenting the instrumentation as he developed his ideas. Time was running out, and Mingus began to panic at the size of the band he had created. He demanded that Knepper write out some of the parts for him. Knepper pointed out that whilst he was a fair trombonist, he was not a mind reader. Cutting the discussion short, Mingus swung a fist and knocked a cap off one of Knepper's teeth. It was unacceptable behaviour at the best of times, but when the victim was a trombonist, it was unforgivable.

Equally thoughtless was Mingus's behaviour at a Village Gate concert around this time. The white drummer Herbie Mann was giving an ostentatious display of African drumming. Unimpressed with the spectacle Mingus asked Mann, in a colourfully direct way, what he knew about African drumming, and then picked up a drum, and threw it at the percussionist. Just to round off the evening Mingus then broke a $10,000 microphone over his knee.

Mingus always wore a pocket pistol (a derringer) round his vast neck, like some sort of eccentric ornament. He told friends that it was a lucky charm, and no doubt it was. It is just that it was always loaded with two bullets. However, Mingus was not without self-awareness. At this time he actually committed himself to Bellevue Mental Hospital because he felt he was becoming a danger to himself and to others. The marriage with Celia had broken up and Mingus

A portrait of Charlie Mingus,
photographed in 1960 at the
height of his powers

was in a bad way. One musical result of his sojourn in Bellevue was the sardonic *All the Things You Could Be By Now If Sigmund Freud's Wife Was Your Mother*, a number whose title poked fun at the psychiatric profession, but which also mocked its composer's volatile personality.

In fact, Mingus's sense of humour was his saving grace and he had a good line in musical send-ups. *My Jelly Roll Soul* parodied the self-obsession of the New Orleans pianist, while Fats Waller's huge appetite, a phenomenon on Mingus was uniquely well equipped to comment, was the subject of a jaunty number called *Eat That Chicken*. He used humour in his stage act too. Faced with a classic drunk at the Village Gate, who asked for *Melancholy Baby*, Mingus immediately obliged, going into a send-up mode which the whole band followed. Of course the drunk loved the deliberately corny performance and gave Mingus a ten-dollar bill. The bassist held it up in front of the audience before tearing it up and trampling it underfoot.

It is a truism to say that Mingus was not an easy man to work for, or to live with. His third wife, Judy, who was a young white woman, would have testified to this: she decided to leave him almost as soon as they were married. But most of the musicians who suffered under his leadership would grudgingly admit that he was, in some perverse way, getting the best out of them. The records were evidence of this. It was the period which produced *Tijuana Moods*, *Mingus Ah Um*, and *Blues and Roots*. Despite the complexity of the compositions on these wonderful LPs, Mingus was in the habit of forbidding his players to write anything down. For those like Danny Richmond with an instinctive understanding of the mercurial leader, this was no problem. But for newcomers finding a way through the changes and reprises, it could be terrifying. Mingus made his instrumentalists struggle to play. At other times he got carried away, explaining the music in such detail that he left almost no time for rehearsal.

In 1962 Mingus teamed up with Max Roach again to record an intriguing LP called *Money Jungle* which featured Duke Ellington on piano as the third member of the trio. Duke was well into the grand-old-man phase of his career and faced with the ambitions of the drummer and bassist, he became defensive. When Mingus suggested something 'really avant garde' Duke's response was 'Oh no Charles, let's not go back that far'. Ellington accounted for himself well on the

LP but Mingus stole the show with his rich melodic runs, and the masterly way he implied the beat without actually stating it.

The 1960s saw the emergence of an exciting new voice on the New York jazz scene. The alto-saxophonist Ornette Coleman, began to liberate the music completely from pulse, rhythm and conventional harmony, and by doing so he challenged Mingus's pre-eminence as an innovator. Mingus was well aware of the threat Coleman posed, because the altoist used to play at a club called The Showplace, just a few blocks from the Five Spot in Greenwich Village which featured Mingus's groups on a regular basis. Keen avant-gardists would shuttle from one club to the other to compare notes on the two men. Coleman was an intellectually formidable player who had established a group of loyal musicians around him, including trumpeter Don Cherry and bassist Charlie Haden. Mingus responded to Coleman's challenge by hiring another iconoclastic reed man who would bring a new edge to his own innovations. It was Eric Dolphy, a hugely gifted alto-sax and bass clarinet specialist. Unfortunately, although he was well on the way to matching Coleman's inventiveness, he died unexpectedly in 1964, due to a chronic diabetes-related condition that had never been properly diagnosed. Danny Richmond thought that Dolphy and Mingus had a close but odd relationship. He said, 'There was not a lot of conversation; at times it seemed as though Charles disliked him but at the same time it was also the feeling that he loved him dearly. And there were times when they duelled musically with each other on the bandstand. So that at Eric's death I know that it affected Charles very, very deeply. I have a feeling that there was something left unsaid between the two of them.'

As black protest grew, with marches in the south (*above*) and riots in Harlem (*right*), Mingus helped the cause with some angry and explicit music.

It is unlikely that two such strong musical personalities would have had totally converging musical aims, and after Dolphy's death, Mingus, mindful of the way he had used the saxophonist principally to trump Coleman's threat, was perhaps oppressed by a sense of guilt. The arbitrary and meaningless way Dolphy died, did nothing to assuage Mingus's sense of anger and outrage. As the sixties progressed, his anger was to take a more overtly political form.

There had always been a civil rights element in jazz, even before the phrase was coined. After all, jazz was a music developed by former slaves, combining African and European traditions to great creative effect. For the earliest musicians, the assertion of black pride was subconscious but palpable. Duke Ellington made it explicit in pieces such as *Black Beauty* dedicated to the memory of the famous singer, Florence Mills. He was of a generation and a class for whom explicit militancy seemed coarse and counter-productive. Lester Young evaded the issue as long as he could, while Charlie Parker for all his anger, was too unfocused and ill-disciplined a social creature to make any serious contribution to the race issue.

Mingus was ready to support the cause of the burgeoning civil rights movement with his music and as the marches, protests and sit-ins polarized the southern states, one of his compositions *Fables of Faubus* with its chanted taunts against the notoriously racist Governor of Arkansas, became an unofficial hymn of some of the more militant activists.

On a personal level, Mingus' anger was fuelled by being evicted from his New York apartment by the City authorities for late payment of rent. The event was captured by documentary-maker, Tom Reichman, in a short film which he called simply, 'Mingus'. The crippling contradictions in Charles' character were vividly conveyed. One minute he was firing into the ceiling with a shotgun, the next embracing his five-year old with real tenderness and consideration. A few months earlier he had been living in an elegant apartment in Sutton Place. It seemed that like Charlie Parker, he had a deep-seated self-destructive instinct which descended upon him whenever he was within reach of material or emotional security.

Deliverance was at hand when Mingus married for the fourth and final time. Susan Graham was white, like Judy, and came from a sophisticated background. She confronted rather than excused his anger. It might have been an easier option for her to feed it with talk of racism, but by standing up to what she saw as his unacceptable personal behaviour she earned his respect and love.

Having established himself as the leading exponent of ensemble jazz, Mingus found old colleagues were drifting back into the band to augment the new talent he was unearthing, so the 1970s started in a very promising way. Then tragedy struck. As the decade progressed, it became clear that Mingus was ill. He was eventually diagnosed as suffering from Amytrophic Lateral Sclerosis. It was a wasting disease that first weakened this great bull of a man, confined him to a wheelchair, then silenced and finally killed him.

The odd thing about Mingus's reaction to the illness was that it was so calm. After years of blowing up at the slightest thing, he faced his fate with resignation and humour. It is almost as if the anger he felt throughout his life had an element of clairvoyance in it. Once illness struck him, the unfocused and sometimes incoherent rage abated. As Mingus's condition declined it was increasingly painful for close friends like Danny Richmond to witness.

Mingus performed musically until virtually the end of his life, latterly from a wheelchair.

It was so very sad. Charles would sit and talk with me for maybe ten minutes, and then he'd suddenly say, 'Well, ah, Danny I've got to go and take some medicine and I'm going to rest, I'll see you later.' And it turned out that every time I went to see him the time kept getting shorter and shorter, that it would be maybe only a matter of minutes that he would say, 'I have to go.' It was very, very hard for me and without Mingus saying it, I could look in his eyes and feel that it was even harder for him.

He still managed to direct the band and play the bass from his wheelchair, and one of his last records featured his old Boss Lionel Hampton on vibraphones. The title track was Mingus's *Duke Ellington's Sound of Love*, an elegiac tribute to the master who about fifty years earlier, had inspired the six-year-old Charlie to start playing music. It was a sort of closing of the circle.

Ironically, Mingus's musical stature was not officially recognized by mainstream America until he was desperately ill. A guest at Jimmy Carter's White House in 1978, Mingus was so moved by the event, and so hurt by the way fate had withheld it until it was almost too late, that he wept uncontrollably. It was a very different scene from the one a few years earlier when a sprightly Richard Nixon welcomed Duke Ellington on the occasion of Duke's seventieth birthday.

While they were in Washington, Mingus and his wife met the baritone saxophonist Gerry Mulligan who had been spending a lot of time in Mexico. Mulligan had taken an interest in Indian medicine, and recommended a remarkable eighty-year-old woman healer whom he thought might be able to help Charles. So Mingus and Susan took off to Mexico in search of healers, shamans and mediums. It did not work, but Susan retained happy memories of the trip: 'It was the best possible thing we could have done. We spent six months in Mexico with some kind of hope, and Mingus keeping everyone's spirits up driving all over the place, looking for the best restaurants everywhere.' He died in January 1979.

By using his band like an artist uses colour in his palette, treating it like a complex instrument and using it to think with, Mingus resembled the man he admired the most, Duke Ellington. The bassist brought back to modern jazz the rich texture and variety of sound that had been so eroded by the rather predictable formula of be-bop: play the tune, solo number one, solo number two, drum flourish, play the tune to close. Despite his fierce emotions, or perhaps because of them, Mingus created a more complex structure as a way of controlling feeling. He re-invented some of the formal devices of Morton, using bridges, interludes and trios. This emphasis on form was, in a way, like a poet turning his back on the brilliant confessional verse of Charlie Parker's solos, and going back to rhyme and metre. It meant that modern jazz was freed from its obsession with iconoclasm for its own sake and became more purposeful and more rooted.

9

John Coltrane playing tenor
saxophone, his eyes closed
in concentration

*Playing with 'trane was such an exhilarating
experience, it was unique, and the presence of it
was so strong that one had to be reverent about
it. And I think for that reason we were all very
close, we loved each other dearly.*

Elvin Jones, drummer, in 1986

John Coltrane

John Coltrane and Miles Davis were both born in 1926, only six years
after Charlie Parker, yet neither of them thought of themselves as
contemporaries of the highly precocious Bird. They belonged to a
younger generation, one that saw the be-bop revolution as a natural
base camp for their musical explorations. Neither Coltrane nor Davis
would be satisfied with the rather dry recreations of the bop idiom
perpetrated by Sonny Stitt and others in the 1950s. The sentimental
glorification of be-bop purveyed by Dizzy Gillespie during long
stretches of his later career did not appeal to them either. In fact, they
came to think of Dizzy as a one-man be-bop revival movement – a
sort of Bunk Johnson of Minton's.

Davis and Coltrane came together in the 1950s to make several
highly influential records under Miles's leadership, but when they
parted company their musical paths diverged sharply. Coltrane
established himself on the challenging heights of the avant garde, and
his work was spiced with eastern philosophy and clouded in
mysticism. Davis was to outlive Coltrane by more than twenty years,
and impatient with what he perceived as the obscurity of jazz in the
1960s, tried to make the music more accessible during the 1970s
and 80s.

John Coltrane was born in the town of Hamlet, North Carolina,
but shortly after John's birth his father's business as a tailor took the
family to Philadelphia. The lively east coast city which was close to
New York and the jazz scene, provided a congenial base for Coltrane
as he grew up and developed an aptitude for music. He started to
learn on the clarinet, moving on to the alto saxophone during his last
year at high school.

Then World War II intervened and Coltrane was called up to join
the navy. His experience of military life was distinctly more benign
than that of Lester Young, for Hawaii was his none too daunting
posting, and John's natural taciturnity and good manners kept him
out of trouble. He even got to play in the US Navy band on the

island, reverting to the clarinet to do so. The war years negotiated without trauma, Coltrane went back to Philadelphia quietly determined to forge a career in jazz. From the start he adopted the serious-minded and painstaking approach that would characterize his attitude to the music. He listened to Stravinsky and Poulenc, and transcribed solos by Parker and Young, so that he could study their structure. Many studious hours were spent in Philadelphia Library with Jimmy Heath, Coltrane's contemporary and fellow saxophonist, trying to unravel the secrets of jazz.

Coltrane, like Heath, was playing alto saxophone at this time. They were both, by definition, in awe of Charlie Parker whose dazzling technical brilliance was reaching its height in the late 1940s. Perhaps Coltrane intuited that a change of instrument was called for if he was to find his voice in jazz. In any case he took the opportunity to join up with Eddie 'Cleanhead' Vinson's blues band in 1947, in which he was required to play tenor. He spent an enjoyable nine months on the road with the sleek, shiny-skulled blues singer.

Coltrane's first big break meant a temporary return to the alto saxophone. It was an offer to join Dizzy Gillespie. Dizzy, Parker's major co-conspirator in the be-bop revolution, had formed a big band which specialized in Cuban idioms as a way of colouring the tempos and harmonies of be-bop. Cuban music and its relationship to jazz was a lifelong interest of the aimiable trumpeter. The effect of a big band playing fast be-bop themes, if exciting, was slightly ungainly. Dizzy's outfit had a strangely futuristic, striving, machine-age sound that was distinctly eccentric. It was the last in a line of under-documented and under-recorded outfits that took big band jazz from Kansas City idioms to be-bop idioms – Jay McShann, Earl Hines, and Billy Eckstein were Dizzy's predecessors – and provided invaluable work for musicians like Gillespie, Parker, and Coltrane himself in their early years.

For Coltrane, the big band arrangements were a chance to shine at reading and transcribing – all those hours of study in the Philadelphia Library had not been wasted. But like many big band leaders in the post-war era, Gillespie found that as expenses spiralled, it became impossible to carry on. What is more the Gillespie big band had not been received with universal rapture. At one concert in Arkansas there were more people on stage than in the audience. So Dizzy formed a quintet, and John Coltrane not only managed to find his way into the group, but also secured the tenor saxophone chair. He was to stay with tenor for the rest of his career, augmenting it with important work on the soprano sax, but never again returning to Charlie Parker's alto territory.

Coltrane's work with the Gillespie quintet began to show his taste for the difficult in music. The aspiring, almost ominous style that was to characterize his work was already well developed. It was a very different sound from the deceptively effortless lucidity of Lester Young at his pre-war best; different too from the sumptuous solos of Coleman Hawkins which were still essentially rooted in the melodies of the 1920s and the 1930s.

John was a tall, serious-looking young man who habitually leaned forward as if trying to catch what was being said to him. Quiet, thoughtful and introspective, he was popular with everyone, especially dentists. He had a compulsive desire for anything sweet he could lay his hands on – what was left of his teeth was appalling to behold and other musicians were at a loss to know how such a serious-minded saxophonist could do such a thing to himself. But somehow Coltrane coped, and even when the time came for major dental surgery his playing was apparently unaffected.

Coltrane playing with trumpeter Lee Morgan when they were both in the Dizzy Gillespie Orchestra in the late 1940s

After the Gillespie experience, the 1950s went slowly for him. He was in and out of various uninspiring rhythm and blues outfits. Not that Coltrane, for all his burgeoning interest in the cutting edge of jazz, was a musical snob. When the chance came to join Earl Bostic's rabble rousing band, which used the rhythm and blues idiom more effectively than most, John jumped at it. But a more promising opportunity was just around the corner. The great altoist, Johnny Hodges, had left the Ellington Band taking a few of the Duke's other stars with him, and formed his own orchestra. Hodges offered Coltrane a seat in the saxophone section, and it was accepted with alacrity. After years of working with Duke, Hodges was attempting to find his own musical voice. Unfortunately, he discovered that freedom from Ellington was not to be the release for which he had hoped. It turned out to be a bitter demonstration of how much his own brilliant instrumental work depended on the Ellington ambience to nourish it. Coltrane's work with Hodges appeared to suffer from his leader's failure to find a voice for his band. But the root of John's problems at this time were not so much musical as pharmaceutical.

During his time with Hodges, and no one really knows why, Coltrane became a heroin addict, a cross he chose to bear for about four years. He functioned on a daily level and even managed to maintain his equable easy-going manner, but the heroin made him musically erratic, and the 'clean' Hodges felt moved to let him go. Luckily though, in 1955, Miles Davis needed a tenor player to replace Sonny Rollins and the trumpeter came knocking on Coltrane's door. It is difficult to judge whether Davis's own kicking of a serious drug habit not long before, made him more or less tolerant of such misdemeanours among his sidemen. At the time he hired Coltrane, his band comprised Red Garland on piano, Paul Chambers on bass and Philly Jo Jones on drums, all of whom were on heroin. It was known as the J & B band – the junk and booze band.

As both soloist and composer, Miles had a crisp, laconic style that was at the opposite end of the spectrum from Coltrane's prolix tenor playing. It might be imagined that Davis would have an instinctive antipathy to John's style, but he was an enlightened leader and gave Coltrane the freedom to develop his 'sheets of sound'.

Around this time, John married a Muslim from Philadelphia called Naima. Her quiet faith, which helped her stand up to the pressures produced by his drug habit, must have been influential in broadening John's cultural and religious horizons. But his addiction was, if anything, getting more serious, and at the end of 1956 he was fired from the Davis quintet.

There followed a period with the spiky, brilliant pianist Thelonius Monk which inspired the finest playing in John's career to date. An incident in a mid-1957 recording session shows what difficulties Coltrane's heroin addiction had got him into. The band were playing *Well, You Needn't*, and high on junk, John was dozing off in the studio. Monk reached the end of his piano solo and was about to cue Coltrane when he looked up and saw him, eyes closed, nursing his sax in his lap. From the keyboard Monk shouted, 'Coltrane, Coltrane!' and the saxophonist stood up like an automaton, played a perfectly articulated solo, sat back down again and nodded back off to sleep. Monk's desperate cry is preserved on the recording.

Later in 1957 Monk and Coltrane went on to play a residency of legendary brilliance at the Five Spot in New York. The pitch of creativity was such that a moment's loss of concentration meant musical oblivion. As John put it, 'once lost, it was like walking into an empty lift shaft'. Monk's habit of dancing on stage during other people's solos only added to the extraordinary drama. The Five Spot was packed, and Coltrane's collaborators-to-be, Elvin Jones and Archie Shepp, were in the audience night after night, enthralled by what they heard.

It seems likely that the very demands of the time with Monk convinced Coltrane that if he did not kick the drug habit he would be finished as a musician. Certainly it was in 1957 that he turned his back on heroin forever. Just for good measure he went teetotal at the same time, and was never to touch another drop of alcohol. During the intensely religious period at the end of his life, Coltrane often referred to 1957 as the year of his spiritual awakening.

The association of drugs and jazz is a cliché often used to add spice to the image of the music as some sort of underworld art, as if heroin addiction were fun. But it would be wrong to dismiss the connection between drugs and jazz as a stereotype with no basis in reality. While it is true that some highly influential jazz men were moderate drinkers and never touched anything stronger than aspirin, King Oliver and Duke Ellington among them, it would be pointless to deny that serious drug abuse did penetrate jazz culture deeply and damagingly.

The brilliance of pianist Thelonius Monk, here playing in a New York loft in 1968, was a great inspiration to Coltrane during the 1950s.

It is not unique to jazz of course. Whenever art has put a premium on the visionary rather than on formal perfection, drugs have played a part. Poets as diverse as Baudelaire, Coleridge and Rimbaud used opium to further their creativity. Jazz is not necessarily visionary in that sense, but improvisational composition night after night in public, in an ambiance where mistakes or even mediocrity were unacceptable, was an extremely demanding experience. Heroin provided long-lasting 'highs' of great lucidity, with none of the debilitating disfunctional effects of alcohol. Furthermore, the negative effects of heroin, now widely known, were less frequently acknowledged in the fifties and sixties. Nevertheless, it is surprising that someone as disciplined and austere as John Coltrane, or as self-confident as Miles Davis should start on heroin.

Some have blamed the Mafia for targeting the black community and pushing hard drugs into Harlem after World War II. The novelist and playwright James Baldwin once told me his theory which was even more sinister. He blamed the State for dumping drugs in the ghetto as some sort of malign social experiment. He added darkly 'I make that accusation and I dare anyone, dare anyone to call me on

it.' Paranoid though Baldwin's notion may sound, the outbreak of the
hard drug habit in Harlem was remarkably sudden. It raced through
the black community like a forest fire, destroying families, community
support systems, and social structures.

Jazz music is, to some extent, a reflection of the stimulants or
abstinences that sustained its musicians. There is something of the loud
conviviality of alcohol about New Orleans jazz, while the dreaming
fantasies of Lester Young smack of marijuana. Be-bop reflects the
frantic dislocation of heroin, while the later work of Coltrane seems
powered by an ardent asceticism and a quest for spiritual purity.

By renouncing drugs in 1957 Coltrane wanted to set a new tone
and to take jazz out of the shadow of destructive dependencies. And
in this respect he succeeded magnificently. Despite the horrors of the
ghetto crack wars, jazz musicians have now, for the most part, turned
their backs on drugs: these days a shot of bourbon against the winter
cold, or a thirst-quenching beer in summer are more typical pre-
concert stimulants.

After his withdrawal period had passed, Coltrane emerged buoyant
and with something to prove – not least to Miles Davis, the leader
who had let John go a year earlier because of his addiction. He
rejoined Davis for what was to be one of the most productive periods
in the trumpeter's career. The seminal LP *Milestones* provided an
interesting example of Coltrane's continuing search for difficulty. In
the tune *Two Bass Hit* he deliberately chose to solo in D Flat because
it was a difficult key, eschewed by many of his colleagues. For John, it
was a matter of honour to make it sound as natural as the key of C.
Coltrane's tenor style lacked the natural elegance of Lester Young's,
and often the long asymmetrical phrases he developed impressed more
by dint of their intensity of feeling than by their inherent musicality.

The problem of Coltrane's prolixity resurfaced in a more acute
form than it took during his first stint with Davis, because altoist
Cannonball Adderley had joined the group, and solo space was at a
premium. At an Apollo Theatre concert, Coltrane was blowing away,
eyes closed and oblivious to everything for about fifteen minutes.
When the number was over Davis went up to him and asked him why
he had gone on so long. 'I couldn't find anything good to stop on,'
said John. 'All you gotta do is take the horn out of your mouth,'
explained Miles, thoughtfully.

John Coltrane playing the soprano sax, the instument on which he recorded much of his finest work

While working with Davis on *Milestones* and *Kind of Blue* Coltrane also began recording under his own name. Indeed the sheer volume of work he undertook in 1958 was evidence in itself of his newly 'cleaned up' state. The success of his LP *Giant Steps* convinced him that the time was right to go his own way. The record was hailed as a major landmark in jazz history, although in retrospect it sounds rather dry, with its ostentatious and self-conscious complexity. Coltrane's real breakthrough as a leader, however, came when he took a break from the tenor and moved to soprano saxophone.

This instrument had come back into fashion partly because Sidney Bechet's achievements on it were being reassessed following his death

in 1959. It had a beguiling, almost Islamic tone that was well suited
to the oriental philosophies that were beginning to interest Coltrane.
The soprano led him to try out Indian scales and African repeating
figures. He experimented with harmonics using the mouthpiece to
produce two notes at once.

The 1960s announced themselves with a rich burgeoning of
experimental jazz. Ornette Coleman's free-form experiments, Eric
Dolphy's work with Mingus, Albert Ayler, John Gilmore – they were
all pushing forward the frontiers of the music in different ways.
Coltrane, with his inquisitive mind and appetite for achieving what
was difficult, wanted to do the same.

The group he assembled to meet this challenge was one of the finest
jazz quartets ever. Joining Coltrane on soprano sax were the brilliant
pianist McCoy Tyner, the Detroit-born drummer Elvin Jones, and
bassist Jimmy Garrison. Instead of scrambling tunes and coming up
with something unrecognizable like the be-boppers, or going into
improvisational free-fall like Eric Dolphy, Coltrane decided for the
moment to stick with the structures and harmonies of American
popular songs as his raw material. But, perhaps under the influence of
McCoy Tyner, he looked further than the standard tunes that had
served jazzmen in the 1940s and 50s until they were virtually threadbare.

The result was to create another example of the exhilarating
tension between form and content that so often powered jazz music.
In *My Favourite Things*, Coltrane and the quartet deconstruct the
sanguine ditty from *The Sound of Music* in a brilliantly sustained piece
of musical argument that is also inherently witty. Julie Andrews would
hardly have recognized the oriental fervour of Coltrane's choruses, or
the rich African web of Elvin Jones's percussion. This recording
session was the final occasion when jazz on the cutting edge worked
its magic on American popular song. Afterwards, modernists
including Coltrane himself turned their backs on tin pan alley as a
source of musical material, thus ending a sixty-year-old tradition.

Elvin Jones recalled these times with deep affection verging on awe
– the musical rapport was such that the group never had to rehearse.
Indeed, they avoided talking about the music lest articulating their
feelings about it in words broke the spell of creativity.

My Favourite Things was Coltrane's last recording on the Atlantic
label. His growing stature in the jazz world had won him a new

The great quartet formed in 1961: McCoy Tyner at the piano, Coltrane, Jimmy Garrison on bass and Elvin Jones on drums

contract with Impulse, where he teamed up with a highly sympathetic recording manager called Bob Thiele. Thiele was moved by the musical and spiritual odyssey Coltrane was embarked upon and did everything possible to shield him from the pressures exerted by some of the more conservatively minded executives at Impulse. In fact, in many ways Thiele was to the avant-garde musicians of the 1960s what John Hammond had been to the emerging swing bands in the 1940s. At the time, Coltrane's friend, the poet Le Roi Jones (now Amiri Baraka) paid Thiele the ultimate compliment by saying that he knew several black record executives who would not have put themselves on the line for Coltrane the way Bob did. Thiele, like John Hammond, was white.

One way Thiele found of protecting Coltrane from pressures within Impulse and also from the adverse criticism that generally greets the strenuously avant garde, was to persuade him to diversify a little and record some more familiar material, thus exposing him to a wider audience. In 1962 there was a record with Duke Ellington which by definition lent Coltrane some credibility among the jazz establishment. There followed an LP called simply *Ballads*, in which Coltrane, back on the tenor saxophone, simply played the tunes and yet managed to stamp his own musical personality on them. John went on to work with a vocalist, Johnny Hartmann, producing a sumptuous album in which songs like Billy Strayhorn's *Lush Life* and

Martin Luther King leads
a civil rights march through
Alabama in 1965. Although
Coltrane's music was not
explicitly political, he hinted
at his sympathies in pieces
like *Alabama*, recorded
in 1966.

You Are Too Beautiful seemed like the still centre of the whirlwind of experimental creativity that was engulfing him.

He was also extending his spiritual and philosophical interests with a magpie-like voracity, and his metaphysical interests made him increasingly impatient with what he considered the entirely parochial matter of racial politics in America. Coltrane never turned his back on the Civil Rights Movement, as pieces like *Alabama* demonstrate; he just took a wider view, according to which a sort of transcendental spiritual awakening would render meaningless the question of colour. Certainly Coltrane was taking a different stance to the struggles of the 1960s from that of the more earthy and militant Charles Mingus.

On a personal level, the marriage with Naima, having survived the ordeal of John's heroin addiction, had broken down. Around 1963 John met a promising young pianist from Detroit called Alice McCleod, who was soon to become Mrs Coltrane and produce three sons. Naturally enough she also had ambitions to become the quartet's pianist.

The first really explicit manifestation of John's profound, pantheistic feelings about religion came with the LP *A Love Supreme*. It was followed by *Ascension*, in which the great quartet was joined by seven other players including Pharaoh Sanders and Archie Shepp on tenor saxophones. The session took the form of a free-form blow that, as Bob Thiele said, 'scared the hell out of me'. All he knew in advance was that the band was going to play for about thirty minutes. *Ascension* sounds at times like a musical primal scream, but the musicianship of the players and the strength of Coltrane's feelings imbue it with a spiritual power which is deeply affecting.

No one who knew Coltrane doubted the seriousness or the sincerity of his philosophy; he was not one of those musicians, for example, who thought that having a sitar in your band automatically made you profound and interesting. But for McCoy Tyner, Elvin Jones and Jimmy Garrison, Coltrane's emphasis on the spiritual was increasingly at the expense of the music. Tyner was the first to go, exhausted by free-form rites of passage and sensing that Alice Coltrane, who shared John's spiritual interests as well as his domestic life, was destined to take over as the band's pianist. Coltrane had meanwhile been studying the spiritual aspects of African percussion. As a result, he decided that the band needed a second drummer to augment and counterpoint Elvin Jones. The inevitable tension that developed between newcomer Rashied Ali, a name guaranteed to meet Coltrane's approval, and Jones was not exactly diffused by what Elvin called Ali's defensive insistence on sitting centre stage and pushing the senior drummer off to one side. Before long Elvin had moved off the bandstand altogether, and joined Ornette Coleman.

McCoy Tyner and Elvin Jones, both Coltrane's peers, were great musicians, whereas Alice Coltrane and Rashied Ali had nothing like their stature, and by hiring them Coltrane showed himself to be too much at the mercy of his philosophical notions. The fact that Alice was also his wife probably made any sort of discussion along those lines within the group awkward to deal with.

There is a whiff of 'spritual correctness' hanging around Coltrane in these closing years of his life. The LP *Cosmic Music* provides a fairly good example of how the post-quartet music was developing. On a track called *The Sun*, Coltrane and Pharoah Sanders repeat the following invocation:

May there be peace and love and perfection
throughout all creation,
May there be peace and love and perfection
throughout all creation …

Coltrane in contemplative mood towards the end of his life, looking not unlike the Buddha to whose teachings he adhered

This buddhistic feeling bore a surprising resemblance to Louis Armstrong's almost contemporary *Wonderful World* in which birds in the trees were really singing 'I love you …' In a curious way Coltrane's transcendental avant-garde exploration seemed to have brought him full circle back to the minstrel tradition of Armstrong.

By 1966, Coltrane was suffering from liver problems, a distant inheritance from his drinking and drugging days. His last LP *Expression* used the eerie arabesques of the soprano saxophone to great effect, hinting at imminent death and somehow anticipating the spiritual afterlife that Coltrane had prepared himself so ardently for.

When he died in 1967, John Coltrane's pantheistic philosophy and peace mongering were already being taken up by white hippies in San Francisco, and his oriental interests were being popularized (some would say vulgarized) by John Lennon and Yoko Ono. Perhaps Coltrane was delighted, and felt that his beliefs about the universality of spiritual truth were somehow vindicated. But where did his late experiments leave the music? Despite the power of *Ascension* and *Expression* his was a highly esoteric and fiercely demanding idiom that was undoubtedly alienating much of jazz's natural constituency. On the other hand, as pure innovation, Ornette Coleman's experiments with harmonics and rhythm which predated Coltrane's avant-garde phase, seem to have been more radical and more influential.

In other words there is a danger that Coltrane's reputation may rest more on the perceived eccentricity of the spiritual beliefs he held late in life, than on the inherent value of his music. This impression is strengthened by a visit to the One Mind Evolutionary Transitional Church of Christ, in a run-down area of San Francisco. The odd Christian sect that worships there have taken John Coltrane as a sort of latterday patron saint. The liturgy combines the Book of Common Prayer with chants from *A Love Supreme* and informal dance and meditation sessions based on the music from *Sun Ship* and similar records. Devotees talk of 'Coltrane consciousness', and the love of Christ expressed through John's music. Admirable though all this may be on a pastoral level, it is difficult to resist the conclusion that some of Coltrane's late music drifted too far from the mainstream of jazz to sustain itself as jazz.

Something of John Coltrane's personal integrity came across in his music though. Whether it was the striving tenor solos on the *Milestones* LP, the majesterial soprano work on *My Favourite Things* or the delicate, sinuous minimalism of *Expression*, Coltrane at his best could match the finest jazz ever played.

IO

Miles Davis photographed at
his final concert in 1991 with
guitarist Joseph McCreary

*For me the urgency to play and create music
today is worse than when I started. It's more
intense. It's like a curse ... and I love that it
hasn't abandoned me. I feel really blessed.*

Miles Davis, in his 1989 autobiography

Miles Davis

Before his latterday incarnation as an avatar of jazz rock fusion, Miles's work had been associated with a style of jazz known as 'cool'. In fact, it was thought that Miles invented this way of playing: that he was responsible, as the title of one of his LPs rather portentously put it, for the 'Birth of Cool'.

Miles Davis in New York before he developed his taste for outlandish clothes

In fact, there had always been a cool style of jazz, the most notable early exponent being the white trumpeter Bix Beiderbecke. The way Bix distanced himself from the material he was playing, the relaxed lyrical phrasing and the propensity for slow tempos, these were the marks of a 'cool' player. Recording and performing conditions in the 1920s were not conducive to this style, however. Indeed the predominantly hot style of early jazz could be attributed in part to the way musicians had to fight to make themselves heard first in noisy halls and then in primitive recording studios.

Things had changed by the time Lester Young made his small group recordings and his style inspired the players who formed the Cool School as such in the early 1950s. While Lester's rhythmic and melodic ideas influenced the be-boppers, the sound he produced from the tenor saxophone, implying reticence and extreme relaxation, led in a different direction. In other words, the aspect of Lester's style derived from his days as a teenage drummer produced be-bop while his Frankie Trumbauer-influenced tone spawned the Cool School.

If Miles Davis formalized the idea of the 'cool' out of these precedents, it was as a result of his reaction against the hectic complexity of be-bop. Although he was impressed and excited by the iconoclastic stance of the be-boppers, as an instrumentalist the style never really suited him. In some ways he was no more sympathetic to be-bop than Charles Mingus, but being just a bit younger and therefore more respectful of the east-coast ambience that Parker had created, Miles decided to cosy up to the be-boppers at the beginning of his career.

Be-bop trumpeters, like Dizzy Gillespie who relished Parker's swift tempos, had cut their teeth in fast and furious big bands where loud playing was essential. It was a sound that had its origins in the fierce, brassy sounds of the Basie Band. But Miles came from a different tradition, in which the trumpet could be lyrical, contemplative and moody. It was a tradition well represented in St Louis where Miles was raised, and as a young man he heard Clarke Terry and Shorty Baker playing just such a style. In fact, Terry who went on to play a significant part in the Duke Ellington story, was a friend of Miles's trumpet teacher.

Miles was born in Alton, Illinois in 1926, but his parents moved to East St Louis almost immediately, the same East St Louis that was so majestically evoked by Duke Ellington in his masterpiece that was first recorded in the year of Miles's birth. Miles Davis Senior came from one of the very few black families which had managed to establish themselves in modest commercial activity after the emancipation, and had then gone on to accumulate wealth and social standing. He was justifiably proud of his lineage, and passed on his pride to his son. Miles's father was a dentist, and he and his wife were dedicated to giving their son the best possible upbringing. On their East St Louis estate, Miles could play and ride horses in total security. Both his parents were musical and his father was particularly keen on jazz.

Bix Beiderbecke, the great trumpeter who in some ways anticipated Miles's 'Cool' style

It was a much more privileged upbringing than that enjoyed by Duke Ellington, but similar in its inculcation of black pride and self-sufficiency. The chemistry of its interaction with Miles's personality was very different, however. Instead of producing Duke's relaxed and polite self-confidence, it conjured up a broody, at times chippy aggression, where pride shaded off into arrogance. This might have been because East St Louis was an aggressively red-necked town, and the Davis household did not enjoy the sanctuary of the close-knit and sophisticated black community that sustained the Ellingtons in Washington, DC.

Miles Davis often adopted an anti-white pose during his career. The fact that some of his closest musical associates – Gil Evans, Keith Jarrett, Dave Holland – were white, indicates that it was probably just a pose. But the anger that fuelled it was real enough, and it may have had its origins in the sense of isolation engendered by living in East St Louis.

On his thirteenth birthday Miles received a trumpet from his father, and started to play in the high school band. He had private lessons from Edward Buchanan, a gifted teacher and keen observer of the jazz scene. But before long Miles found that trivial music competitions put on by his school were rigged so that inferior white players could take the first prize.

Miles was lucky: Buchanan was in a position to introduce him to one of his heroes, Clarke Terry. The young man soon discovered that there was a simple physical explanation for the broad, warm tone that characterized Terry's playing. He used a deeply cut Heim mouthpiece. It also tended to limit him to the middle register, as it made high notes quite inaccessible. Davis emulated Terry's use of the Heim, and stayed with it for the rest of his life.

In his early teens Miles listened to the first recordings Parker made with the McShann band and some examples of Dizzy Gillespie's work. These records spoke of an uncompromising energy and musical radicalism that made the St Louis scene seem staid and provincial. Davis sensed the be-bop revolution was coming, and he was determined to be a part of it. When the Billy Eckstein Band came to St Louis with Parker, Gillespie and other notable modernists in its ranks, Miles made sure he was around to see what was going on. At the first rehearsal he discovered that the trumpeter Buddy Anderson had just been diagnosed as consumptive, and was being sent home to Oklahoma City. Miles volunteered his services and sat in for him with alacrity. Thus while still a high school boy, he had his first experience of the big time.

He was proving precocious in other ways too. At the age of sixteen a hasty marriage caused his parents much dismay. What is more, they had hoped for a medical career for their son, with music as a hobby. It was becoming clear that Miles would major in music. His medical interest would prove to be limited to the pharmaceutical imperatives that afflicted the be-bop generation, but that would be long after he left St Louis.

In 1945 Miles went to New York to study at the Juillard School of Music. He took his academic career seriously, but not his need for sleep, as he spent his evenings and nights trying to locate Charlie Parker. Having cut loose from Eckstein, and graduated from Minton's, Bird had just established himself at the Fifty-second Street Club, The Three Deuces. Davis was nineteen years old and he was ready to make a Faustian pact with Parker in order to be in the right place at the right time. He intuited tensions between Parker and Gillespie, both of whom coveted the be-bop crown, and he thought that he could exploit the conflict. He was right – before long he was playing alongside Parker at The Three Deuces. And when the first historical recording of a be-bop quintet was made by Savoy later that year, it was Davis, not Gillespie, who was Parker's first-choice trumpeter.

Miles's work on this session was uncertain and nervous, but his burry, warm tone distinguished him from Gillespie, and gave the ensemble passages a distinctive tonal colour. Davis's laconic, static style held its own in the slow numbers, but he was rather overawed by the whole experience, and for the up-tempo compositions, he stood down. Dizzy Gillespie was on hand to play on *Ko Ko* and *Thriving on a Riff*, and he did so with his usual power and skill at hitting extremely high notes.

Davis could match neither Gillespie's power nor his high notes, partly because of his Heim mouthpiece, but basically because he was not physically equipped to do so. As he matured he never overcame, nor sought to overcome the physical limitations of his playing It has been said that Miles made a trumpet style out of hitting the wrong notes, which is not really fair, but there was always the hint of technical fragility in his playing. On the 1945 Savoy session there were fluffs, but also a burgeoning musicality which rescued the nineteen-year-old from disaster.

Davis seems to have been rather obsessed with Parker at this time. Hearing of Bird's trip to California in 1946, he took a job with the Benny Carter Band specifically because Los Angeles was on their itinerary. On the west coast Miles rode himself in on the small group recordings made by Dial. Parker came to the studio with complicated arrangements in his head and nothing on paper. Davis struggled with the new material and consequently sounded tentative and unfocused in his solos.

With Bird's breakdown and confinement in Camarillo, Miles found himself stranded in California without work and without Parker. He had got a ride to the west coast with Benny Carter's Band and it was another outfit which rescued him from an unwelcome stay in Los Angeles. Billy Eckstein's Band was playing out its final weeks down there, and Miles joined up to travel back to New York with them.

Miles playing at the Three
Deuces in New York in
1948 with Charlie Parker.
Miles was twenty-two.

It was there that the Parker Quintet was reformed on Bird's return from California. Miles stayed with Parker for about twenty months, and the group recorded for both Dial and Savoy. Miles's confidence as an instrumentalist was growing and on slow numbers like *Embraceable You* and *My Old Flame*, he produced lyrical solos of great elegiac beauty. But Parker's behaviour was beginning to rile Miles. One of Bird's infantile tricks was to introduce Davis, and then let off a balloon into the microphone. The fact that Miles had always worshipped Bird seemed reason enough for the saxophonist to humiliate him publicly. But Davis' stature was growing, and in 1947 he won the *Down Beat* magazine new star award, and realized that he did not have to take this sort of thing, even from Charlie Parker. He quit.

In any case it had become clear that the predominantly fast and furious be-bop style did not suit Miles temperamentally. And there was more to this creative dissonance than just metronome speeds. While he was still with Parker, Miles had been approached by the white Canadian pianist composer Gil Evans, who wanted to arrange the Davis composition *Sippin' at Bells* for the Claude Thornhill Band. Miles released the rights to Evans, and became fascinated by the Canadian's work.

Evans was the man who had smuggled records and whisky to Lester Young during the tenor player's solitary confinement in an army barracks two years earlier. Building on his youthful admiration of Duke Ellington's subtle orchestrating skills, Evans had developed his own unique palette of sounds, which were influenced by Richard Strauss and Schoenberg. He was the first jazz musician to free himself from the notion that the beat had to be marked in an explicit way. Evans described his music as 'hanging like a cloud' and against contemplative backgrounds he set expressive and energetic solo parts. He composed like a jazz improviser, and Miles was intrigued by the subtle multi-layered sound that Evans created for Thornhill's Band, which had started life sounding more like Glenn Miller than anything else. Davis started to borrow scores so that he could study Evans's approach. Having left Parker he was working with a group that included the trombonist, Kai Winding at New York's Royal Roost. Miles had the idea of putting together a medium-sized jazz ensemble incorporating some of his current sidemen, and using the skills of Evans as an arranger. He managed to persuade the people at the Royal

Roost that this was a good idea, and a two-week residency was arranged. More remarkably, Davis convinced Capitol that they should record two sessions with the ensemble after the residency was over. It was not a band with irresistible commercial clout, but with the recording ban just over, the feeling among the big record companies was that anything black, vinyl and circular would do.

Thus began the first collaboration of Miles Davis and Gil Evans, a partnership of the highest distinction that produced some very subtle and sophisticated jazz. The instrumentation of the Capitol sessions indicated the originality of the approach Evans and Davis were taking. To Miles's trumpet were added trombone, french horn, tuba, alto and baritone saxophones. The rhythm section of drums, bass and piano comprised a different personnel for each session and called on the services of both Max Roach and Kenny Clarke. One of the pianists was John Lewis, the scholarly musician who had played on the Parker's Mood session, and who would go on to found the Modern Jazz Quartet, a group dedicated to purveying the most refined and delicate chamber jazz.

The exquisite overlapping textures of Evans's arrangements, like sunlight glittering on a calm sea, provided a beguiling background for sudden darts of individual exuberance. The most dissonant note in any chord was often given to the french horn, the softest of the wind instruments in the ensemble. This, together with the early Ellingtonian absence of the tenor saxophone with its strong middle register created a mood of astringent mystery. The numbers *Israel* and *Moonbeams* are among the masterpieces of jazz.

And yet the residency was a flop and the recordings a commercial disaster. For once the old argument about music being ahead of its time seems to have been justified. The music of the Capitol sessions was also difficult to classify. Its relaxed mode of presentation and rhythmic reticence left listeners used to the assault and battery of be-bop puzzled. The commercial failure of the Capitol session embittered Davis, who felt that a new and highly creative jazz idiom had sunk without trace. He experimented with an even bigger band using Tadd Dameron as arranger and with Red Rodney and Zoot Sims in its ranks. The sole survivor of the Capitol Sessions was trombonist Kai Winding. But it was an experiment that did not succeed. Even the most established big bands were finding it hard to survive after the war, and Davis's advanced ideas had little chance of making themselves heard. He had established himself as a creative leader, but had achieved little or no success in that role.

He was also troubled by the way a Cool School had been formalized on the west coast. A group of mainly white musicians led by Lee Tristano and Gerry Mulligan had developed Miles's ideas to produce a jazz style that was verging on the glacial. They acknowledged Miles as the founder of their movement, but he felt they had somehow hijacked the music and emptied it of its meaning. In short, the early fifties found Miles confused and struggling to find work. As a middle-class student he had steered clear of the be-bop heroin habit, but faced with a hiatus in his career and with his teenage marriage on the rocks, he swiftly declined into addiction. There followed a few patchy years when Davis lacked direction and was playing uncertainly.

A New York recording sesssion with Capitol graduate Lee Konitz, who had become one of the gurus of the Cool, was not a success. Davis sounded diffident and unconvincing, and on one number *Ezz Thetic* he backed out of the difficult ensemble passage, hastily improvising an easier supporting part in the background. Never a virtuoso, Miles was in danger of losing his credibility as a competent technician in any sense.

The session served only to reinforce Miles's convictions that he had to distance himself from the 'cool' approach. Big band and ensemble work were not for the moment an option, especially when so much of his energy was taken up with scrabbling around for heroin. What he needed was a different sort of small group sound, one that would contrast with his own instrumental approach. When he teamed up with tenor saxophonist Sonny Rollins in 1951, the portents were good. Rollins was only twenty-one but had a rich tone and an articulate attack rooted in the be-bop tradition. Their recordings were uneven though, with Miles often sounding more like an addict than a leader. However, when he remade one of his favourite tunes *My Old Flame* some of Miles's fire and aesthetic poise came through.

While still working with Rollins, Davis found time to undertake a date for the Prestige record company with Charlie Parker who was billed as Charlie Chan, for contractual reasons. It was notable as being one of the very rare occasions when Parker recorded on tenor. On this occasion, their earlier roles were reversed, with Davis the leader and Parker the sideman. However, Miles did not use the occasion to take revenge on his erstwhile mentor and humiliator and the session went surprisingly smoothly. Which was more than could be said for a disastrous record date with Thelonius Monk which brought the prickly trumpeter and the reclusive pianist to the verge of exchanging blows. At one point Davis refused to play if Monk accompanied him. Thelonius did not comply with the leader's instructions to shut up but he did tone down his highly personal style so that it suited Miles's lead better. It was a compromise of sorts, but the rift between the two men was never healed.

When Davis later recorded Monk's *Around Midnight* in the mid sixties the opening was chaotic, his solo started with a false note and then proceeded in what sounded like a deliberately incompetent way. It is difficult to avoid the conclusion that this was Davis's long-contemplated revenge on Monk. Why else should he have allowed such a poor rendition to be pressed?

Miles's clash with Monk was followed three years later by a similar clash between the morally resolute, musically demanding pianist and

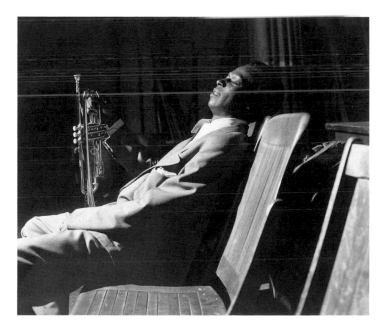

Miles Davis, resting between takes in a 1950 recording session

John Coltrane. It was to unsettle Coltrane and contribute to his decision to give up his hard drug habit. Whether the exigencies of the Monk session had caused Miles to reach a similar conclusion or whether he simply recognized that to work effectively he had to kick heroin, he decided that the time had come to go 'cold turkey'. When he emerged 'clean' in 1954, aged twenty-eight, he was ready to embark on the most creative period of his career.

Davis had secured a long-term contract to play at Birdland and needed to find a replacement for Sonny Rollins, who had gone off on one of his lengthy and silent sabbaticals. Miles took a chance on the virtually unknown John Coltrane, partly because of the saxophonist's seriousness and ambition. There followed a period of consolidation for Davis when he showed considerable skills as a leader, moulding his inexperienced quintet together and encouraging Coltrane, despite the often severe criticism his tenor playing provoked.

Miles's own solos were also gelling as never before, and his mature style was beginning to articulate itself. He eschewed the theatrical climax-building of the traditional jazz solo, and the more oblique drama of the be-bop solo. Instead, he favoured a sort of anti-climactic dying fall so that his solos faded like a beautiful sunset. Numbers such as *There is No Greater Love* and *When I Fall in Love* contain solos that articulated this approach beautifully and the structural embodiment of Miles's interest in the 'cool' approach was all the more effective when it contrasted strongly and effectively with the loud and distinctly 'uncool' playing of the rest of his quintet. Davis's frequent use of the mute emphasized the lyricism of his approach and created a feeling of tension and excitement. However, the anticlimactic solo was a high-risk enterprise – one misjudgement and it might sound merely bathetic.

With his career buzzing, Miles's taste for beautiful women and fast cars was a frequent subject for the gossip columnists. He was also something of a fashion icon. Whether kitted out in expensive Harris tweed or black leather trousers, he generally looked very good. He kept in trim by boxing, which also seemed to release some of the aggression that was pent up inside him. Miles's features were strikingly fine, and his bright eyes often burned with anger, an anger that satisfied the expectations of white liberals. He played the trumpet with his spine curved backwards in a taut arc and his hips thrust forward.

Opposite, Miles Davis at the Paris Jazz Festival. His wardrobe was often as impressive as his playing.

Generally he turned his back on the audience and never announced a
number or acknowledged applause. Occasionally his gravelly almost
inaudible voice could be heard giving a clipped instruction to some
anxious sideman. Miles was the embodiment of a sort of 1950s hip
which was not without its own vanity.

Much has been made of his surliness towards audiences, but this
was perhaps the least objectionable of his traits, and was his reaction
against what he saw as the obsequious and demeaning flattery of the
public purveyed by Louis Armstrong in his later years. It was left for
players of a younger generation to be both polite and uncompromising in front of an audience – players such as Ornette Coleman
and McCoy Tyner.

By the time Davis, maddened by his saxophonist's continuing
heroin addiction, had to let Coltrane go in 1956, he was established as
an international star with considerable commercial clout. He decided
to use that clout to resuscitate the ensemble jazz project he had
undertaken with Gil Evans six years earlier. When Miles gave him a
call, Evans was freelancing in relative obscurity in New York, so he
took the opportunity to throw himself into the revived collaboration
with great enthusiasm.

In May 1957, they recorded *Miles Ahead* using a nineteen-piece
orchestra which was a logical enlargement of the Capitol ensemble.
Miles played the flugelhorn, which has a slightly lower register than a
trumpet. It suited his smoky, ominous tone beautifully. This
magnificent record showed Miles at his most controlled, backed by
Evans's brilliant arrangements that set off his brooding, smouldering
solos. 'He can read my mind and I can read his' was how Miles paid
compliment to his selfless arranger. The achievement of *Miles Ahead*
was all the more remarkable given wholly inadequate rehearsal time,
and Evans's diffident and unconvincing conducting style which
required heavy interpretation on the part of the instrumentalists.
Long tours of the pre-war type were also not on the agenda – the cost
and the other commitments of band members made such ideas
impracticable, but nevertheless the Davis/Evans big band was making
itself felt as one of the most original and creative voices in jazz.

Miles had heard on the grapevine that Coltrane had kicked his
heroin habit, and the trumpeter knew better than most what a
difference this could make to music-making. He made his peace with

the tenor player and invited him to rejoin his small group which had
been augmented to include Cannonball Adderley on alto. This sextet
produced a seminal pair of LPs, the first of which was *Milestones*.
With its laconic and beguiling use of scales the title number had a
high definition sharpness and clarity that distinguished it from the
turbulent fury of be-bop without becalming it in the increasingly
pallid articulations of the Cool School.

Davis's next project with Gil Evans was a version of Gershwin's
Porgy and Bess. Evans reinterpreted and condensed the opera with his
usual skill and sensitivity using Davis's trumpet to carry the burden
of the major arias. Miles played his heart out on these arrangements
by a white band leader of an opera by a white composer, which had
been attacked for being sentimental about the south and patronizing
to blacks. His reputation as a bigot or a hothead was beginning to
look a little shaky.

Miles's triumphant 1958 was complete when he wrote the score for
the Louis Malle film *L'Ascenseur pour L'échafaud* in which his elegiac
style matched perfectly the gritty lyricism of the French 'new wave'.
He was featured on the cover of *Time* magazine, a confirmation of a
sort that he had captured the imagination of the American public.

Another wonderful record followed. The sextet recorded *Kind of
Blue* in 1959 with the great Bill Evans on piano (another of Miles's
distinguished white colleagues, and no relation to Gil). The date was
produced by the highly sympathetic Teo Macero, a composer in his
own right, and was a model of what a jazz recording session should be.
Davis came to the studio with minimal but lucid arrangements jotted
down, affording maximum freedom to his sidemen. The album was
full of excellent music, and Miles's solo on *So What* reached new
heights of beauty and concision.

The decade which had opened so uncertainly was ending in
triumph. There followed one more collaboration with Evans, the
sumptuous *Sketches of Spain*, the centrepiece of which was a reworking
of Rodrigo's piece for guitar and orchestra, *Concierto de Aranjuez*.
Despite the beauty of this version, and the ingenious way Evans's
arrangements made the orchestra sound like a massive guitar, *Sketches
of Spain* was the least successful of their joint efforts. The reworking
of the Rodrigo piece was in the final analysis rather pointless, and
Rodrigo's sombre Iberian mood was somehow too literal a vehicle for

the fugitive shifting melancholy that characterized the best of the
Davis/Evans scores. Another piece on the album, *Saeta* opened with
castanets, and was dangerously close to evoking the Spain of a
thousand tourist brochures.

Miles's magisterial progress through the 1950s was brought to an
end by John Coltrane's chronologically neat decision to leave in 1960
and start his own group. The symbolic significance of his departure
was considerable, because Free Jazz and other types of avant gardism
were making themselves felt around this time. Miles did not doubt
that Coltrane would use his considerable talents to advance
experimental jazz, and suddenly the trumpeter was faced with a choice
of joining the avant garde or heading a musically conservative
rearguard action. Both options were in different ways distasteful to
him. He spent the early years of the 1960s squirming rather
uncomfortably on the horns of this dilemma.

Davis photographed with his
first wife, Francine, in 1961

Davis considered the problem of his replacement tenor player with
almost political scrupulousness. He finally settled on Sonny Stitt, best
known as the altoist to whom Charlie Parker is said to have offered
'the keys of his kingdom' in the last month of his life. Stitt was also a
considerable tenor player. But this partnership was very short-lived.
Miles then hired Hank Mobley, a musician from Georgia who had
played with the Jazz Messengers and Dizzy Gillespie. Mobley was a
good player with a rich tone, but the work he did with Davis was
strangely colourless and lacking in conviction – not surprising,
perhaps, given Davis's state of mind at this time.

The closest Davis got to flirting with the avant garde, was to
agonize about inviting Eric Dolphy into his band. Although a modernist, the reed man had a lyrical, graceful style, and Miles thought
like Mingus, and for similar reasons, that he might be able to do
musical business with him. But he never quite got round to asking
him, and then Dolphy died so unexpectedly. It is difficult to judge
how Dolphy would have ultimately placed himself in relation to the
various modernist movements that were flourishing at the time of his
death. But one thing is certain, like the guitarist Charlie Christian, he
was a great loss to jazz.

In general the modernists irked Miles. When he shared a club date
with Archie Shepp, one of the lions of the avant garde, Davis walked
off the stand, disgusted by what he considered unmusical prolixity.

When quizzed about free jazz he said, 'If something sounds terrible man, a person should have enough respect for his own mind to say it doesn't sound good. It doesn't to me and I'm not going to listen to it.' At the same time, he was anxious to avoid digging himself a bunker as a sort of a latterday old-timer.

In 1963, Davis made some changes to his band. Mobley was replaced by another southern tenor man called George Coleman, who did not really settle either. The really significant newcomers at this time were in the rhythm section. Herbie Hancock, an accomplished player who understood Miles's melodic ideas took over on piano, and Tony Williams, a prodigy from Boston was the new drummer. Both newcomers were young and had impeccable jazz pedigrees, but they were also interested in the world of soul and rock with its mass audiences. For the moment though, with the gifted Ron Carter on bass, they were content to work within Miles's jazz idiom, and to help revive the trumpeter's flagging enthusiasm for the music.

The new quintet gelled with the arrival of Wayne Shorter on tenor saxophone. He had graduated from the Jazz Messengers, where the perceptive Art Blakey had given him opportunities to express himself as a composer as well as a soloist. Shorter's attack was fierce and his musical logic highly developed. Hearing him play was like being confronted by a chess player with a rip saw. The combination of Williams's power and Shorter's fire brought Davis right back to his finest form. Indeed, for what might have been the first time in his career, Miles seemed to be so influenced by his sidemen that he began to shed some of the cool and minimalist aspects of his style. Shorter's zest affected the way Davis attacked his own solos. Nor was the leader grudging about giving the newcomer his due as a composer. Shorter tunes such as *ESP* and *Iris* were recorded as soon as the new quintet got into a studio, and Davis's solos seemed to signal his appreciation of Shorter's compositions.

Shorter was also in broad sympathy with the outlook of Williams and Hancock. Miles was rescued from the inertia of the early 1960s when the young bloods in his quintet presented the middle-aged trumpeter with a way forward that fortuitously avoided the dangers of avant-gardism and reaction.

No sooner was the quintet assembled than Miles had to undergo major surgery on an arthritic hip. Keen to get back to the music-

Art Blakey gave many young musicians a start in his Jazz Messengers. Records like *Free for All*, released in 1957, were highly influential on Davis and others.

Miles with Wayne Shorter
in 1967. Shorter helped
edge the trumpeter towards
'electric' jazz.

making, he left hospital before he should have done, promptly fell and broke the affected leg. After an enforced and frustrating eighteen-month lay-off, he was back in the studio to make the excellent *Miles Smiles*. The last of many LPs to deploy the leader's first name in a punning title, it included Shorter's beautiful composition *Footprints* and a solo by Davis on *Nefertiti* which examined every aspect of the theme for more than eight minutes. Breaking down the melody into fragments, he then developed, reversed and transposed it through many different keys. It was both exhaustive and compelling.

Davis was clearly relishing the tense, powerful jazz to which Shorter and Williams had introduced him. His mute, much in evidence throughout the fifties, often gathered dust as he belted out solos in a new, attacking voice. Miles also developed the technique of playing continuous, integrated one-and-a-half hour sets at concerts. Different themes and compositions were deployed but the band moved from one to another in a well-rehearsed and highly effective musical stream of consciousness. It may have seemed an extreme solution to Miles's notorious reluctance to address an audience, but the dramatic and emotional impact of this approach was undeniable.

The success of the new quintet reduced the threat of the avant garde for Miles. Also the death of John Coltrane in 1967 seemed to mark a symbolic end to the first phase of free jazz experimentation. Miles's reasons for rejecting these approaches were not just musical. He was becoming worried about the way the increasing sophistication of jazz was making it inaccessible to the black youth for whom Miles felt it was important to play. Indeed, his own work with Gil Evans was a prime example of beautiful jazz with an essentially minority appeal, and throughout his career, most of his audiences had been predominantly white. In fact, the esteem in which he was held by the white community sometimes made him uncomfortable. He despised the ingratiating Uncle Tom antics of the older generation of negroes, but suspected that he was offering another version of the same thing. For all his aggressive and surly posturing, he remained an icon of *Time* and *Playboy* magazine and the more he frowned, the better the white liberal establishment liked it. In short, he was an updated, hip avatar of the token negro.

At the same time he was on the receiving end of uncomfortable reminders of the sort of pressure the majority of black Americans were under. At the height of his fame in the late 1950s when he was taking a breath of air between sets at a Birdland concert, a policeman approached him and told him to move on. Miles explained that he was playing at the club. The policeman promptly beat him about the head, threw him in the back of his car and drove him off to the nearest police precinct where he was kept in overnight on some trumped-up charge. Of course, given who he was, when he appeared the next day in court Miles was completely exonerated. But it was painfully obvious to him that anyone else of his colour might not have been so lucky. Ghosts of his St Louis childhood had been revived.

In the late 60s, a feeling of solidarity with black youth, the influence of Shorter, Williams and Hancock and his innate musical instinct led Miles to make a radical change in his approach to jazz. There is no reason to assume that the electric jazz rock fusion that characterized the last phase of his career was played in bad faith as some purists have suggested, but vanity might have had something to do with it. Miles had met the powerful and charismatic guitarist Jimi Hendrix, and something inside him craved the mass adulation that rock stars could command.

Having engaged Miles's interest in the possibilities of jazz rock fusion, Wayne Shorter, Herbie Hancock and Tony Williams left the quintet towards the end of the decade, but Miles went on to produce his first major electric album, *Bitch's Brew* in 1969. Although Davis seemed to have mastered his electric trumpet and wah-wah pedal, the band was inflated by numerous guest instrumentalists and sounded distinctly under-rehearsed. The rhythm section alone boasted up to nine players. If the intention was to convey a feeling of depth and density, it backfired. The effect was of muddiness and imprecision. Miles started to play rock as well as jazz venues, and threw in some massive multi-instrumental climaxes to satisfy the psychedelic and orgiastic expectations of the time. But audiences began to feel that Davis's traditional concision had degenerated into virtual spectatorship: he was playing less and less. Miles had invented a sort of *nouvelle cuisine* of jazz rock fusion, and some people began to feel that despite their complexity and pretension the musical portions on offer were unacceptably small.

In the recording studio, Miles had recourse to multi-track recording and splicing techniques which he used with cavalier abandon to build his increasingly laconic solos up to commercially acceptable durations. Sometimes a solo would just be repeated by the crude means of copying it, and splicing the two pieces of tape together. At other times a previously recorded solo would be used as a background to some new improvisation. It was synthetic and rather careless music.

Davis worked with fine musicians in the seventies: English bassist Dave Holland was virtually ever-present; Chic Corea and the brilliant Keith Jarrett played keyboards, but the predominant impression was that a concern with musical fashion and political correctness had dulled the creative spark of the man who had given the world *Miles Ahead* and *Kind of Blue*.

The problem with Miles's rock fusion experiment is not simply that he did it, as some believed, but that he did not do it very well. Wayne Shorter went off to form the excellent Weather Report, and Herbie Hancock's Headhunters were also a great success. Both these fusion bands were tighter, more inspired and more commercially viable than the electric Davis. In the rock world, Davis was no match for the raw, blues-inspired power of early Hendrix, or the visionary originality of the San Francisco band Grateful Dead. In short, the great jazzman seemed to have misjudged the situation. As the seventies progressed Davis became more and more isolated. In the occasional interview he would angrily disown his finest music, and denounce the whole idea of jazz as a white construct. Any criticism of his electric music was dismissed as garbage.

His health also took a turn for the worse. He had more trouble with his hip, underwent surgery to remove a stomach ulcer and then had to have growths removed from his throat. To make matters worse, he was having a litigious time with the Inland Revenue investigators. By the late 1970s, Davis had become a virtual recluse, sitting in a large brownstone in Harlem, the windows shuttered against the daylight, receiving only the closest friends, and sitting in virtual silence with them for hours at a time.

Gaunt and emaciated, photographed in Nice, 1990, Davis has the air of an African prophet.

Miles's changes of fortune always seemed to coincide with the arrival of a new decade, and in 1980, he presented himself at a specially arranged CBS party and announced he was ready to start work again. In all honesty his work in the 1980s was uneven and intermittent, but the funk idiom he developed had more conviction about it. Also the music was more precise, and a new generation of sidemen, such as George Duke on drums and synthesizer and Michael Urbaniak on violin was making its presence felt.

By this time longevity and persistence were beginning to work in Miles's favour. He appeared at the New Orleans Jazz Festival in 1986 wearing a loose-fitting oriental-looking jacket with matching baggy trousers made out of gold lamé. His hair was thinning and his arms gaunt and boney. The impact of his appearance was rather more memorable than his music.

In 1990, Miles faced a new decade for the last time. Astonishingly, he decided to recreate some of the masterpieces of the Gil Evans era for a concert he gave at the Montreux Jazz Festival. Working with Quincey Jones' Orchestra he embued numbers from *Miles Ahead* and *Porgy and Bess* with a powerful elegiac force. It became apparent that this was the swansong of a great musician remembering some of the high points of his career for the last time. Miles's trumpet-playing was physically weak, but it glowed like a dying ember.

Davis was a man who should be judged more by his actions than by his words. He often complained about white men not being able to play jazz, and yet he enjoyed some of his most creative partnerships with white musicians. He denounced sophisticated jazz and yet produced some of the most subtle and complex sounds any jazz musician had played. As he approached his death in 1991, it was not the synthesized swirl of the seventies and eighties that he implicitly acknowledged, but the rich palette of sounds that he had created with Gil Evans nearly forty years earlier.

II

Ornette Coleman's Free
Jazz, released in 1960,
changed the face of modern
jazz with its ambitious
and risky spontaneity.

*You're never in a secure position. You're never
at a point where you have it all sewn up. You
have to choose to be secure like a stone, or
insecure but able to flow.*

Keith Jarrett, pianist, speaking in 1990

Coleman, Marsalis and Jarrett

The late work of Coltrane and Davis constituted a sort of Scylla and
Charybdis – two dangerous extremes for the jazz musicians of the
next generation. The dangers were of esoteric, arcane mysticism on
the one hand, and the drowning of jazz in the funk and rock idiom
on the other. Coltrane believed that jazz needed spiritual and
intellectual ambitions to survive while Davis thought the music had
to rediscover a mass audience to flourish. Both men were right, of
course, but in the sense that they ignored the dangers implicit in
these contrasting positions, they were wrong as well.

As we have seen, jazz began as a dance music rooted in popular
culture, but from the outset its musical and social aspirations created
a tension between its popularity and its growing sophistication. In
terms of combining originality with mass appeal, the most successful
period of jazz history was arguably the late 1920s, when Armstrong
and Ellington were in full flow. Certainly, the chance jazz had to
command centre stage as a popular art has been swept away by the
emergence of a black musical culture deriving from Motown and
comprising aspects of soul, funk and disco. The relentless beat of the
drum machine seems to have hypnotized the mass audience. It is
ironic that black music has only achieved widespread commercial
recognition and success when it seems to have lost its beauty and
distinctiveness.

Serious jazz musicians working in the 1990s have to come to terms
with the fact that theirs is a musical art with minority appeal. The
best way to keep jazz alive is to bring about innovations that are
informed by a strong consciousness of its roots. A musician who has
succeeded in just such a way is the alto saxophonist Ornette
Coleman. The fiercely demanding idiom of his music belies its
rootedness and vitality, and Coleman's contribution to jazz has been
consistently underrated.

Born in Texas in 1930, he had an obscure and discouraging
apprenticeship, playing in rhythm and blues bands around the south-

west. When he tried out his teenage version of Charlie Parker's alto style he was bawled out and told to play it 'straight'. He gave up the unrewarding musical grind and took an even less promising job as an elevator operator in Los Angeles, so that he could study music theory in his spare time. This he did on his own and with great intensity, coming up with some highly personal interpretations of what harmony meant and how it could work.

When he started playing again, his mature style was virtually fully formed. It was radical in the extreme. He abandoned the idea of a regular pulse and threw out the harmonic scaffolding that jazz had used as a discipline from Bolden onwards. The effects of asymmetry and even arbitrariness were alarming, but for those with ears to hear, Coleman's utterances were deeply coloured by his blues roots. By dispensing with pulse and harmonic progression he was reaching back to the most primitive 'hollers', even before they were yoked to the rhythms of work songs. His frequent use of bowed bass was similarly ambiguous: to some it was evidence of Coleman's real interest in contemporary classical music, but it also harked back to the early era of New Orleans before the bass was plucked.

Like all great players, Coleman developed a highly vocalized instrumental style – in his case, a wailing, strident crying tone which he produced from a plastic alto which, for years, was his preferred instrument.

When Coleman recorded *Free Jazz* in 1960, his project of throwing out both pulse and harmonic progression became widely known, and the reaction it provoked was extraordinarily negative. The hostility was not just on aesthetic grounds – there was a nasty edge to it. Mingus and Coltrane felt that they could divide the kingdom of modern jazz between them, and found no room for Coleman, who was a quiet man and something of an outsider on the east coast scene. Ten years earlier Mingus had been an outsider too, but to his discredit this earlier experience did not make him sympathetic to Coleman's situation.

Coltrane followed Coleman into the free jazz idiom with some impressive work. The difference between them was that while Coltrane's pieces were like meditations, Coleman, although abandoning regular rhythm, often managed to convey a sense of swing. This claim would not be universally supported, even by those

who enjoy Coleman's music. But if it is true, swinging without a
regular pulse was a breakthrough even more significant than Parker
swinging at very high tempo.

In 1962 Coleman stopped playing for three years while he taught
himself the violin and trumpet. He wanted to master instruments
which carried no baggage of association or cliché for him. In his quest
for truly original improvisation he felt that the alto sax offered him
too many instinctive and engrained responses for his own good.

When he revealed his new instruments and new style in 1965 the
volume of abuse directed at him rose to unprecedented heights. At
this time Coleman played with Elvin Jones and Jimmy Garrison lately
of the Coltrane quartet. They were refugees from Coltrane, but not it
seems from modernism. Other notable sidemen have been the bassist
Charlie Haden and Ornette's son, the percussionist Denardo
Coleman. Someone who was associated with Coleman on and
off for about thirty years was the trumpeter Don Cherry. Cherry,
whose favoured instrument remained the pocket cornet, was roundly
abused for the eccentricity of this choice by, among others,
Miles Davis.

Ornette Coleman, playing
his favoured plastic alto

Having cleared his mind with the violin and trumpet experiments,
Ornette has now arrived at a slightly more approachable style. Still
playing beautifully at the age of sixty-four, he favours a simple quartet
with bass and drum backing. His music tends to be more structured
than in the sixties, featuring compositions of great lucidity and
admirable concision, which are both original and yet deeply-rooted in
jazz tradition. He deserves a wider audience, both inside and outside
the jazz fraternity.

One player who has achieved such a wide audience, particularly
amongst the young is the trumpeter Wynton Marsalis. A public,
almost ostentatious cultivation of his New Orleans roots, combined
with an astutely-pitched brand of jazz neoclassicism, seems to have
captured the public imagination. The facts of his early life seem
specially contrived to provide him with the perfect up-market jazz
curriculum vitae. Marsalis was born in the birthplace of jazz in 1961
and swiftly demonstrated a gift for music. At the age of eight he
played in a children's marching band, put together for the New
Orleans Jazz and Heritage Festival. He studied classical trumpet as
well as jazz and performed the Haydn Trumpet Concerto with the

New Orleans Philharmonic when he was just fourteen years old. Unlike Charlie Mingus, he was able to cross the musical rubicon into the classical world, showing that some sort of progress has been made in tearing down the most overt aspects of racial discrimination. Marsalis went on to study at that most prestigious of musical academies, Tanglewood.

Canny talent spotter Art Blakey discovered Marsalis, and the trumpeter's jazz career started with Blakey's Jazz Messengers. Before long he had left to form a group with his brother Branford, who plays the saxophone. In 1982, Wynton became the first artist to receive grammies for both a jazz record and a classical recording in the same year. *I think of One* was the jazz album, and a version of trumpet concertos by Haydn, Hummel and Mozart senior the recording that impressed the classical music world.

Marsalis has made his name with some highly structured jazz suites that utilize the call and response patterns of black church music. He likes to work with the same sort of ensemble that Mingus used in his workshop phase, but the more formal voicing of Marsalis's ensembles recalls Ellington rather than Mingus. The later Ellington of the Sacred Concerts was probably particularly influential.

Marsalis's music is powerful and impressive stuff, rather like the black church services on which it is based, but perhaps it is rather too knowing in its exploitation of its own roots. At times Marsalis seems

Wynton Marsalis on trumpet in 1993

perilously close to a black heritage industry and, indeed, his first
public appearance as a musician at the age of eight, was in just such a
context. His music provides an aural parallel to the gentrification of
the old quarter of New Orleans which has occurred over the last
twenty years. Something has been preserved, but at a cost. In his
concert appearances, Marsalis' manners are impeccable and he is
always perfectly dressed, as if trying to banish forever the spectres of
Charlie Parker and Charles Mingus.

One of his numbers starts with a recitation of the names of some
well-known Louisiana dishes: red beans and rice, chicken gumbo,
crawfish pie and so on. It could be straight out of a New Orleans
cookbook. Disney's rather dubious 'New Orleans: Jazz City' located at
EPCOT in Orlando, Florida, seems momentarily only a stone's
throw away.

The pianist Keith Jarrett is not in a position to romanticize his own
traditions like Marsalis, nor would he if he could. Revealing the
influence of John Coltrane's ambitions, Jarrett once said that he was
seeking a 'universal folk music'. He has taken a less mystical root than

Keith Jarrett in typically
absorbed frame of mind,
recording at Atlantic Studios
in 1971

Coltrane, but the breadth of reference and ambition in his music is both bewildering and inspiring.

Born in Pennsylvania in 1945, Jarrett studied the piano from the age of three. By the time he was seven he had given his first classical recital, but from the beginning improvisation was his passion.

After studying at the Berklee College of Music in Boston, he was heard at an informal jam session by Art Blakey who immediately asked him to join his group. Jarrett stayed with the Messengers for four months before teaming up with the fearsomely avant-garde Charles Lloyd. It was here that he began to make his mark and to refine his jazz idiom. He plays with an intense lyricism and flawless technique. But it is his almost physical coupling with the piano which is so compelling. At times he will stand at the keyboard and sway as if in a high wind; at others he will crouch foetally as if wanting to disappear. There is no showmanship about Jarrett's style: it is sheer musical feeling which leads to such acts.

During his time with Lloyd, Jarrett learned to play soprano saxophone and percussion – which he still does from time to time. A stint with Miles Davis, doubling on electric organ and piano, seems to have been less successful. It left him with a strong dislike of amplified music which has stayed with him ever since.

As a leader Jarrett has generally worked in trios, with Charlie Haden, Paul Motion and Jack de Johnette among his sidemen, but he has also played solo improvisation of great complexity, sometimes lasting up to forty-five minutes. His musical integrity is striking, and the demands he makes on the listener considerable, but by sheer force of musical personality, he manages to command the attention of a large and growing audience. Jarrett's observation that 'You have to choose to be secure like a stone, or insecure but able to flow' expresses the openness of his own mind towards jazz and improvization. His statement could also be applied to jazz music as a genre. Its roots were in a fusion of styles that occurred in a way that no one has fully understood or explained. Ragtime was secure like a stone, jazz was insecure – a fugitive art and an art that flowed. It must continue to thrive on uncertainty and change to live. Jarrett has absorbed the primordial vigour and intensity of jazz, and reinvented it as a universal folk music. That is a considerable achievement and a hopeful sign that jazz can survive and prosper in the twenty-first century.

Postscript

This book opened with a quotation from Ernest Ansermet's perceptive critical remarks about the compositional skills of Sidney Bechet. Such recognition of the value of jazz made by classical musicians is generally pounced on by jazzmen and writers with manic, disproportionate glee. Farewell the smoky club and the ghetto; hello the concert hall. Such reactions are misguided and distorting and they have led to various exaggerated claims about the influence of jazz on mainstream serious music. The complex rhythms of Stravinsky's *Rite of Spring* have even been enlisted as evidence of African influence. Since the ballet was premiered in 1913 such wild notions can be swiftly dismissed.

Black elements did seep into European music before the end of World War I, and Paris was where they had the strongest influence. Eric Satie's *Parade*, played for the first time in 1917 under the baton of Ernest Ansermet, used syncopated rhythms and imitated everyday sounds in much the same way that blues singers had on their guitars. A year later, Stravinsky, who was living in Paris, became interested in black music and asked Ansermet to send him some scores. Stravinsky was enthusiastic: 'Jazz … burst into my life so suddenly, enchanting me by its popular appeal, its freshness and the novel rhythm which so distinctly recalled its Negro origin.' The result was Stravinsky's *Ragtime*. His title was accurate, more so than his use of the word jazz in the comments quoted above because it was *ragtime* that inspired Satie and Stravinsky. The fact that Ansermet could send scores of the music bears this out: it was too early for either of them to have heard jazz as such.

When the new music did make itself felt in Europe shortly afterwards, it was predictable that Paris would again be the musical centre where it would have the strongest impact. A cult of the exotic had already begun in the visual arts with Paul Gauguin's South Seas experience. As Matisse and the Cubists proselytized about negro sculpture, could negro music be far behind? What is more it certainly suited the purposes of French composers to praise jazz after World War I because they were engaged in cultural trench warfare against what they considered the overblown, elephantine German tradition of Wagner, Mahler and Strauss. The informal voicing of the jazz ensemble and its agile rhythmic felicity therefore had strong attractions for composers like Auric and Milhaud.

Milhaud's interest in jazz became more than merely polemical when he escaped to the clubs of Harlem during a trip to New York in 1922. He was thrilled by what he heard and returned to Paris with a suitcase full of Black Swan 'race' records. Before long Diaghilev had hired him to compose the score for a ballet based upon an African legend of the birth of the world, to be designed by Fernand Léger. Milhaud's score with its jazz instrumentation, use of cross rhythms, and blues notes was the first significant example of the jazz idiom to be used in European classical composition. It is not surprising that ballet was the most successful vehicle for European experimentation with that most quintessential dance music, jazz.

A little later, Maurice Ravel began to take an interest in jazz. He had heard it, albeit in a watered-down form at the Boeuf sur le Toit and it was the melodic possibilities of blue notes that fascinated him. Ravel's 1928 Sonata for Piano and Violin used these to great effect, especially in the second movement which opens with the plucked violin imitating the sound of the banjo. The piano also toys with the main beat in a way that shows considerable understanding of jazz rhythms.

French composers in the 1920s used jazz as a way of defining or augmenting their own compositional idiom. Having dabbled in it, however, they tended to move on. So while the impact of jazz in Europe was considerable, it was indirect and rather short-lived. In the USA, Bernstein's own hopes of becoming a new Mozart who would fuse jazz, Broadway and symphonic tradition into a new form of music drama faded, and as he grew older, he increasingly immersed himself in the sumptuous comforts of the German school.

Duke Ellington flirted with the symphony hall more than most jazz musicians, but in his more realistic moments he was able simply to accept jazz gratefully for what it was. Sitting in his none too plush dressing room at the Apollo theatre, Harlem, after finishing a matinee concert, he was visited by a liberal, well-meaning arts journalist who asked: 'Why should you, the greatest composer of the twentieth century have to put up with conditions like this?' Duke delicately raised a weary eyebrow in silent challenge to the patronizing and ill-judged notion that he was more creative than either Bartok or Stravinsky, and replied, 'Lady, that is a complaint that I long ago decided had no future.' Such realistic attitudes must be good for jazz music. It should not aspire to the status of high art, nor should it succumb to the fashions and conventions of pop music. Jazz started as a music of the underdog, almost a protest music. As it developed it became synonymous with individualism and a refusal (sometimes to the extent of being stubborn and stupid) to follow blind convention. It was just these qualities which made jazz so valued in Russia and Poland in the 1970s, as a refuge from the dreary conformity and hypocrisy of communism. In an age when pop music is marketed on a global scale by huge international corporations, and even orchestral conductors are publicized like pop stars, jazz is capable of providing sanctuary once more: this time from the soulless glare of international hype. Jazz can provide intelligent music on a human scale.

Further Reading

One of the problems with jazz bibliography is that the mistakes made by historians and ghost writers tend to get recycled and become 'gospel'. Although all the books listed below are important as evidence, some are by no means entirely reliable as historical documents.

General

Genovese, E. *Roll Jordan Roll* (London, André Deutsch, 1975)

Goddard, C. *Jazz Away from Home* (London, Paddington Press, 1979)

Hodier, A. *Jazz: its Evolution and Essence* (London, Secker and Warburg, 1963)

Kernfeld, B. (ed.) *The New Grove Dictionary of Jazz* (London, Macmillan, 1988)

Buddy Bolden

Marquis, D. *In Search of Buddy Bolden, First Man of Jazz* (New Orleans, Louisiana State University Press, 1993)

Louis Armstrong

Armstrong, L. *Satchmo: My Life in New Orleans* (London, Peter Davies, 1964)

Swing that Music (London, Longmans, 1967)

Collier, J. L. *Louis Armstrong: a Biography* (London, Michael Joseph, 1984)

Jones, M. & Chilton, J. *Louis: the Louis Armstrong Story* (London, Studio Vista, 1971)

Sidney Bechet

Bechet, S. *Treat it Gentle* (London, Cassell, 1960)

Starr, S. F. *Red and Hot: The Fate of Jazz in the Soviet Union* (Oxford, Oxford University Press, 1983)

Duke Ellington

Collier, J. L. *Duke Ellington* (London, Pan Books, 1989)

Dance, S. *The World Of Duke Ellington* (London, Macmillan, 1971)

Ellington, D. *Music is my Mistress* (London, Quartet Books, 1977)

Lester Young

Mcdonough, J. *Lester Young* (from *Giants of Jazz* series; New York, Time Life Inc., 1980)

Russell, R. *Jazz Style in Kansas City and the South West* (Los Angeles, University of California Press, 1970)

Charlie Parker

Reisner, R. *Bird: the Legend of Charlie Parker* (New York, McGibbon and Kee, 1963)

Russell, R. *Bird Lives* (London, Quartet Books, 1973)

Charlie Mingus

Mingus, C. *Beneath the Underdog* (London, Weidenfeld and Nicolson, 1971)

Priestley, B. *Mingus* (London, Quartet Books, 1982)

John Coltrane

Thomas, J. C. *Chasing the Trane* (London, Elm Tree Books, 1970)

Miles Davies

Carr, I. *Miles Davies* (London, Paladin, 1984)

Davis, M. *Miles: the Autobiography* (London, Macmillan, 1990)

Wilmer, V. *As Serious as your Life* (London, Alison and Busby, 1977)

Ornette Coleman

Litweiler, J. *Ornette Coleman: The Harmelodic Life* (London, Quartet Books, 1992)

Keith Jarrett

Carr, I. *Keith Jarrett: The Man and his Music* (London, Grafton Books, 1991)

Selective Discography

The guiding principle of this discography is an attempt to provide information on key recordings and developments mentioned in the text. At the time of going to press there are some unfortunate gaps which I suspect are temporary. Mingus's work is rather badly represented, and recordings of Lester Young's work appear to be in total disarray.

All recordings are on CD unless otherwise stated.

Louis Armstrong

Louis Armstrong and The Blues Singers 1924–30
AFFINITY AFS 1018-6

Louis Armstrong and His Hot Fives and Hot Seven
CLASSICS 585 512J27

Big Bands Volume 1
JSP 305

What A Wonderful World
BLUEBIRD ND 88310

Sidney Bechet

The Chronological Sidney Bechet 1923–26
CLASSICS 583

The Chronological Sidney Bechet 1937–38
CLASSICS 593

Sidney Bechet 1932–43: The Bluebird Sessions
BMG/BLUEBIRD ND 90317

The Sidney Bechet Sessions
STORYVILLE 4028 (LP)

Duke Ellington

Early Ellington 1927–34
RCA Bluebird 86852

The Duke's Men Small Groups Vol 1
Columbia 468618

The Blanton Webster Years
RCA Bluebird 85659

The Great Ellington Units
RCA Bluebird ND 86751

Black, Brown and Beige
RCA Bluebird 86641

At Newport
Columbia 40587

Second Sacred Concert
Prestige P24045

Lester Young

Giants Of Jazz – Lester Young
Time Life STL J13 (LP)

The Quintessential Billy Holiday Vol. 5
CBS 463333

Count Basie
The Original American Decca Recordings
MCA GRP 36112-3

Charlie Parker

Charlie Parker Memorial Vols. 1 & 11
Savoy SV 0101; Savoy SV 0103

The Legendary Dial Masters Vol 1 & 11
Stash ST 23; Stash ST 25

Bird: The Complete Charlie Parker
Verveverve 837141-10

The Quintet Jazz at the Massey Hall
Original Jazz Classics OJC 044

Charlie Mingus

Money Jungle
Blue Note BZ1Y 46398

Reincarnation of a Lovebird
Candid CS 9026

The Clown
Atlantic 790142

The Black Saint & The Sinner Lady
MCA MCAD 5649

Town Hall Concert 1964
Original Jazz Classics OJC 042

John Coltrane

Milestones (Miles Davis)
CBS 460827

Thelonius Monk with John Coltrane
Original Jazz Classics OJC039

Giant Steps
Atlantic 781337- 2

My Favourite Things
Atlantic 782346 2

Ballads
MCA MCAD 5885

A Love Supreme
MCA DMCL 1648

Ascension
IMPULSE GRD 21132

Expression
IMPULSE MCA 254646

Miles Davis

Charlie Parker Memorial Vols 1 & 11
(includes Miles's early work with 'Bird')
SAVOY SV 0101; SAVOY SV 0103

The Legendary Dial Masters Vols 1 & 11
(Charlie Parker; includes Miles's early work with 'Bird')
STASH ST 23; STASH ST 25

'Miles' Original Jazz Classics
OJC 006

Birth of the Cool
CAPITOL CDP 792862

Miles Ahead
CBS 46060

Milestones
CBS 460827

Porgy and Bess
CBS 450985

Kind Of Blue
CBS 32109

Sketches of Spain
CBS 460604

Cookin' at The Plugged Nickel
COLUMBIA CK 40645

Tutu
WARNER BROS 925 490

Miles & Quincey
Live at Montreux
WARNER BROS 9362 45 22 12

Ornette Coleman

Free Jazz
ATLANTIC SD 1364

At the Golden Circle, Stockholm
BLUE NOTE BCT 84224/5

Wynton Marsalis

The Majesty of The Blues
COLUMBIA CK 45091

Keith Jarrett

Facing You
ECM 1017

Solo concerts
ECM 1035/6/7

Expectations
COLUMBIA 46702

Index

Page numbers in italics refer to picture captions

Photographic Acknowledgements

Archiv für Kunst und Geschichte, London: 115
BFI/Majestic in association with United Artists: 69
From: 'The Cover Art of Blue Note Records', ed. Graham Marsh, Glyn Callingham and Felix Cromey (London, Collins & Brown): 215
Hulton Deutsch Collection, London: 16–17, 51
Library of Congress, Washington, DC: 7
Magnum Photos Ltd: 2, 191, 211, 219
Marquis Jazz Enterprises, New Orleans: 25, 27, 28–9, 39t+b

Musée national d'art moderne, CNACGP, Paris (from Matisse, Jazz, 1943–7): 161l+r
Range Pictures Ltd, London: 8, 11, 21, 72, 83, 100, 109, 110b, 111b, 130, 131, 145, 156, 164l, 178–9, 181l+r, 196, 201
Ray's Jazz Shop, Shaftesbury Avenue, London: 221
Redferns, London/William Gottlieb: 137b, 159/Mick Hutson: 199/Max Jones: 43l+r, 56, 58, 62, 93t, 99, 110t, 111t, 114, 200/Marc Marnie: 225/David Redfern: 41, 73, 119, 123r, 124, 125, 183, 193, 214, 216, 224/Charles Stewart: 185, 197/Bob Willoughby: 70, 209
Rex Features Ltd, London: 164r
Duncan Schiedt: 14, 48, 50t, 78, 80, 89, 90, 93b, 95, 106, 127, 132, 136, 137t, 138, 151, 154–5, 166, 171, 175, 188, 195, 204–5
Universal/Courtesy of the Kobal Collection, London: 86–7
William Ransom Hogan Jazz Archive, Tulane University Library: 18, 32, 50b, 54–5, 91
Val Wilmer: 169, 226; Val Wilmer Collection/Daniel Filipacchi: 143